after reading his *Travel Diary*. *Black Spring* published in June.

1937 Momentous meeting with Lawrence Durrell. *Scenario* published with illustration by Abe Rattner. Began publication of *The Booster* and *Delta* with Alfred Perlès. Went to London during the winter for a few weeks to visit Perlès. Met W. T. Symons, T. S. Eliot, and Dylan Thomas.

1938 Began writing for French revue, Volontés in January, the publication month of *Money and How It Gets That Way*. Second edition of *Alf* appeared in June; *Max and the White Phagocytes* published in September.

1939 *Tropic of Capricorn* published in February, and the *Hamlet* letters with Michael Fraenkel later in year. Left Villa Seurat in June for sabbatical year's vacation. End of a very important period of close association with Anaïs Nin, Alfred Perlès, Michael Fraenkel, Hans Reichel, Abe Rattner, David Edgar, Conrad Moricand, Georges Pelorson, Henri Fluchère, et al. Toured southern France. Left for Athens on July 14, arriving at Durrell's home in Corfu, Greece, in August. Back and forth to Athens several times, visited some of the islands, toured the Peloponnesus. High water mark in life's adventures thus far. Met George C. Katsimbalis (the Colossus); George Seferiades, the poet; Ghika, the painter, et al. Found real home, real climate. Source of regular income stopped with death of Paris publisher (Jack Kahane, the Obelisk Press) the day after war was declared.

1940 Returned to New York in February where I met Sherwood Anderson and John Dos Passos. Stayed with John and Flo Dudley at Caresse Crosby's home in Bowling Green, Va. during the summer. Wrote *The Colossus of Maroussi*, *The World of Sex*, *Quiet Days in Clichy* and began *The Rosy Crucifixion*.

1941 Made tour of U.S.A. accompanied part of the way by Abraham Rattner, the painter, from October 20, 1940 until October 9, 1941. Met Dr. Marion Souchon, Weeks Hall, Swami Prabhavananda, Alfred Stieglitz, Ferdinand Léger and John Marin. Father died while I was in Mississippi and I returned to New York. Left for California in June 1942. Continued with *The Rosy Crucifixion* (finished half of it) and with *The Air-Conditioned Nightmare* (finished about two-thirds).

1943 Made two to three hundred water colors. Exhibited at Beverly Glen (The Green House), American Contemporary Gallery, Hollywood, with success.

1944 Exhibited water colors at Santa Barbara Museum of Art and in London. Seventeen or more titles edited for publication in England and America. Year of fulfillment and realization. First "successful" year from material standpoint in whole life. Was called to Brooklyn in October due to illness of mother. Visited Herbert F. West at Dartmouth College, New Hampshire, and exhibited at Yale. Married Janina M. Lepska in Denver, Colorado, December 18, 1944. Moved to Big Sur, my first real home in America. Emil White arrived in May from Alaska to offer his services. Met Jean Page Wharton, who had a great influence on my thinking.

1945 Finished *Sexus* at Keith Evans' cabin, Partington Ridge. Started translation, which was never finished, of *Season in Hell*. Daughter Valentine born November 19. Bezalel Schatz, Israeli painter, arrived December 26 (my birthday).

1946 Moved to shack at Anderson Creek in January. Began work on *Into the Night Life* book with Schatz. Also began book about Rimbaud: *The Time of the Assassins*. Met Leon Shamroy who eventually bought over 30 of my water colors. Received news from Paris that 40,000 dollars had accumulated to my credit and which I neglected to collect. Jean Wharton offered us her home on Partington Ridge, to pay for whenever we could.

1947 Took possession of Wharton's house on Ridge in February. Began writing *Plexus*. *Into the Night Life* book completed.

1948 Wrote *The Smile at the Foot of the Ladder*. Son Tony born August 28.

My Life and Times

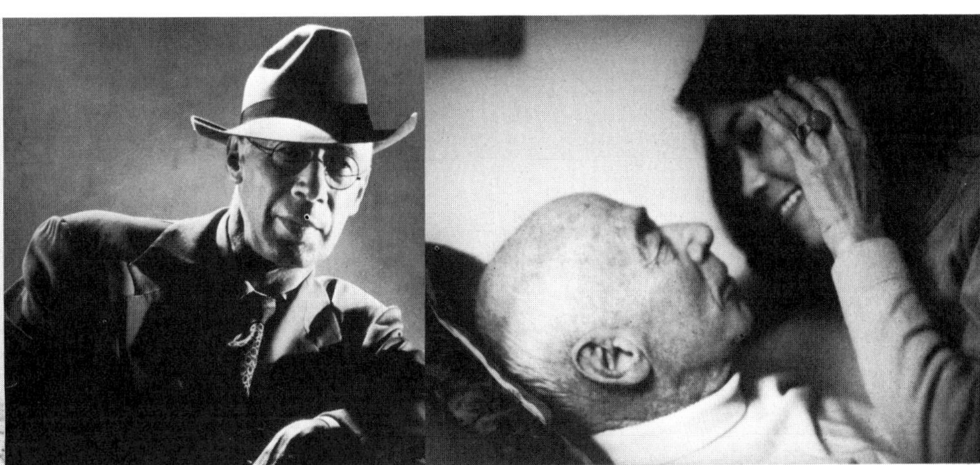

by Henry Miller

My Life and Times

A Gemini Smith Book

by Henry Miller

PLAYBOY PRESS

Library of Congress Catalog Number 75-151843

Printed in Japan.

Created and Produced by Bradley Smith
Designed by Nicole de Jurenev

Production Supervision by Sandra K. Kunze
Research by Helen Paula Smith and
Connie Perry
Printed in Japan by Toppan Printing Co., Ltd.
Jacket Photograph by Bradley Smith
Jacket Drawing by Signor Piero Fornasetti
This book was set on the linotype in Century
Expanded by A-1 Typographers, Inc.

When I asked Henry Miller to write a preface for his book, his first reaction was that prefaces were a chore, a nuisance and a waste of time. But then he expanded on this, saying, "I wrote many prefaces and for very different books—and the only reason for a preface is to help the reader understand and appreciate the book—why don't you write it?" This then is the service I hope to perform in explaining how this book was created.

First you should know how pleasant the hours were to me as Henry retold the story of his life. He had a kindly way of complaining from time to time about the hundreds of hours we worked and he often asked whether we were ever going to get it finished. But the single hours, and even the total year and a half that we labored intermittently on the book, went by swiftly for me and I suspect they did for Henry too.

This account of Miller's life was talked out word by word over many a gin and tonic, many a good French, Italian or Japanese dinner, washed down with bottle after bottle of the liquid combination of sunshine and grapes that comes from the justly celebrated vineyards of France. Our talks, which were prologues to the hours spent in the conversations that were put on tape, were invariably interrupted. No matter which restaurant we selected, no matter how quietly we slipped in and dined in a corner, there were always Miller admirers, from teen-agers to octogenarians, who soon spotted him. Many of them were content with surreptitious looks and whispers across their table—"that's Henry Miller." But there were always some who couldn't resist the impulse to come over and tell him how much he had changed their lives for the better. Many of them expressed their gratitude for the feeling of liberation that Henry had inspired. Henry was always polite, even gracious and gallant, especially with the women. But between admirers I can remember distinctly Henry saying, "This is the way it always is. I'm suffering for all the writing I've done." Yet I could see that he enjoyed the comments of his admirers.

During dinner Henry often commented on our work and progress. As I remembered it, he'd sometimes say, "Bradley, I wonder how it all started, how I let myself get seduced into all this fucking work." Well, this is the way it was. I was editing a book and hoped to have Lawrence Durrell write the preface. I needed

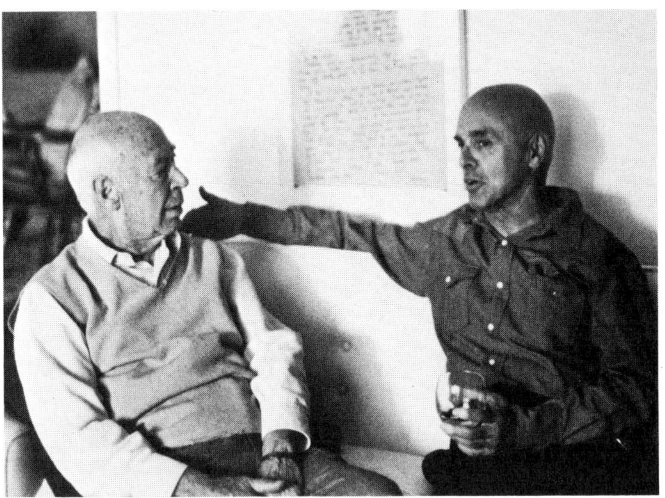

Durrell's address. My friend Helen, now my wife, thought she knew how to obtain it. So she invited a friend of hers, Robert Snyder, the Academy Award film maker (*The Titan—Michelangelo*, *Pablo Casals*, etc.) to dine with us. Snyder was not too sure of Durrell's address but suggested that, if anyone could provide it, Henry Miller could. But by the time he introduced me to Henry, a few weeks later, the deadline for the preface had come and gone.

Far more important to me than anyone's address was news of Snyder's exciting new film, *The Henry Miller Odyssey*. The film was then in production and has since been finished and released. It is a full length documentary

treatment of Miller, his past and present, with Henry himself as the star. Snyder's idea was to give the public an opportunity to see and hear the man whom he considers the most important writer of our time. He has produced a film of lasting value.

As Snyder discussed his film that evening, I began to visualize a different kind of project —a book that would reveal Miller's life in text and pictures—a visual autobiography. When I mentioned this to Snyder, he expressed his willingness to cooperate by making some of the interviews contained in the film available, as well as some of the stills that he had taken on location. I gratefully accepted his offer and a few of the passages were transcribed from the sound track and incorporated into the text of the book.

When I first suggested a visual autobiography to Miller, he said, "But I just finished making a motion picture of my life. Besides, I have written the story of my life in my books as no writer has." When I objected saying that a book was not a *film* and that I hoped to have him retell the story of his life, he reluctantly agreed.

So we began to create an illustrated history of the life and times of Henry Miller as a book. We found out early that we were quite *simpatico* and our conversations were like continuous explorations into the reality of the past. I devised questions that would give a narrative life-line to the book. But while I was doing this I was also planning the visual impressions that I wanted to give of Henry and his friends.

For the next 18 months we talked about Henry's life—his life today, the earlier days in Big Sur and in Paris and New York. Our dialogues included questions and answers about writing, painting, life and death. At more or less regular intervals, Henry got pretty tired of it. As the sun began to set he often said, "Isn't it time for a gin and tonic? Let's end it right here." But we didn't. The dialogues, which became monologues, continued. Sometimes he objected to, but seemed to enjoy, our discussions of intimate aspects of his present life together with some phases of the past which, he said, he never intended to reveal.

I was quite clear about my reasons for wanting to do this book but I asked Henry to comment on his reasons for going along with me. This is what he said:

"The readers may wonder, since my writings are largely about myself, why I should go to the trouble of rehashing that saga of my life in this fashion. I am not sure I can give a convincing answer to the question, except to say that through conversation, or what the French better call *entretiens*, one often approaches a subject or theme from a different angle. Stripped of literary pretentions or flourishes, the facts and events of one's life emerge more starkly and thus, to many readers, more intelligibly and comprehensibly.

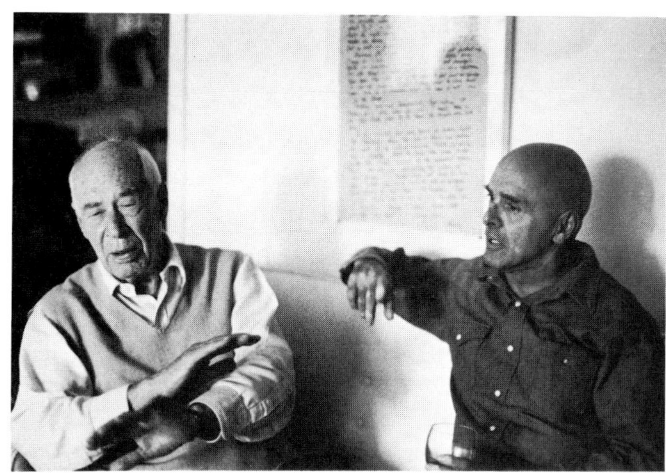

"As it was with the dialogues, so it was with the photographs. Both Bradley and I wanted to include many of my water colors in color—so he photographed them. He also followed me around the house with a camera in one hand and a gin and tonic in the other taking many of the pictures that lend spice and novelty to the text. Sometimes I think they reflect me even better than my own words. In addition to those pictures taken by Bradley, others were dug up from friends, other photographers, library archives, family albums, and God only knows where.

"As I reflect on all these efforts, all this activity, what amazes me more and more is that there can never be a complete, definitive edition of one's life, whether through talk, writing, pictures or analytical probings. All are attempts, explorations, kaleidoscopic constructs—made at given times, in certain moods or in psychological climates which vary greatly. No one method, nor even all combined, ever get "it," which is to say the elusive mystery which underlies everyone's life. The life of even the humblest man, particularly his inner life, is replete with incident and drama beyond all imagination. But if the all is impossible, enough is herein recorded to give a taste of what happened to me in the short space of seventy-nine years."

As the year slipped by I came to know Henry better and to develop a deep affection and respect for him. We played ping-pong together and he invariably won. He wins over most of his guests partly, perhaps, because he plays every day on his own grounds and partly because of his extraordinary reflexes and agility. We were able to talk at home with few interruptions for Henry refuses to answer the telephone. Guests rarely arrive uninvited and the three Japanese girls, his wife and two others, who lived with him, were like shadows in the background. I shall never forget one pleasant accompaniment to our conversations. One of Henry's friends, a young Japanese girl, was studying opera. She was a soprano, and I'm sure I shall never be able to hear the famous *Un Bel Di* aria from *Madama Butterfly* without recalling the aura of the Miller household.

So the California days and nights slipped easily by—sun, smog, fog, sun. While we were in the early stages of the book, Robert Snyder's film, *The Henry Miller Odyssey*, opened to excellent reviews. Then, as the pressure from film-making subsided, Henry had more time for the editing and rewriting of the book.

One day he drove down from Los Angeles to La Jolla to visit me and to write captions for the many pictures in his neat and legible longhand. With that final task the book was finished. We talked about old and new times, we drank and we dined and, because of the excitement of having Henry Miller in the house, my 16 year old step-daughter Janet broke two glasses, one plate, spilled the wine and knocked over a floor lamp.

BRADLEY SMITH
LA JOLLA, CALIFORNIA

To the person who thinks with his head life is a comedy. To those who think with their feelings, or work through their feelings, life is a tragedy.

NOW

I will begin by saying that the way I spend most of my time is not at all the way I would like to spend it. It's because I am still a man with a conscience—which I am sorry about. I am a man who has a regard for his obligations and duties, and these are the things I've been fighting against most of my life. I want to say fuck it all, fuck you all, get out of my life. That's how I feel. I would like, I've repeated it again and again, as far as possible to do nothing, and I mean absolutely nothing. Vegetate almost. Of course it isn't vegetating in the usual sense, but to me it means inactivity, it means a disregard for what people think is important. My emphasis in the last twenty years is in moving from doing to being. I am more interested in being than doing. There is nothing that I really want to accomplish, nothing has any real value to me. Nothing is so important that it has to be done and yet every day I find myself doing these fucking chores imposed upon me by other people. There are so many projects. Everybody thinks he's got to know what I'm doing, what is my life like, what has it been and so on. And I'm utterly disgusted in a way, rehashing everything about my own life or future projects.

I don't want any plans, I have no real plans for the future. Every day when I wake up I want to say *"le bel aujourd'hui,"* as they say in France, and there shouldn't be anything more to it. I want to live the day in whatever fashion I like, and I have no fashion. I'm at that wonderful, beautiful point where I don't see

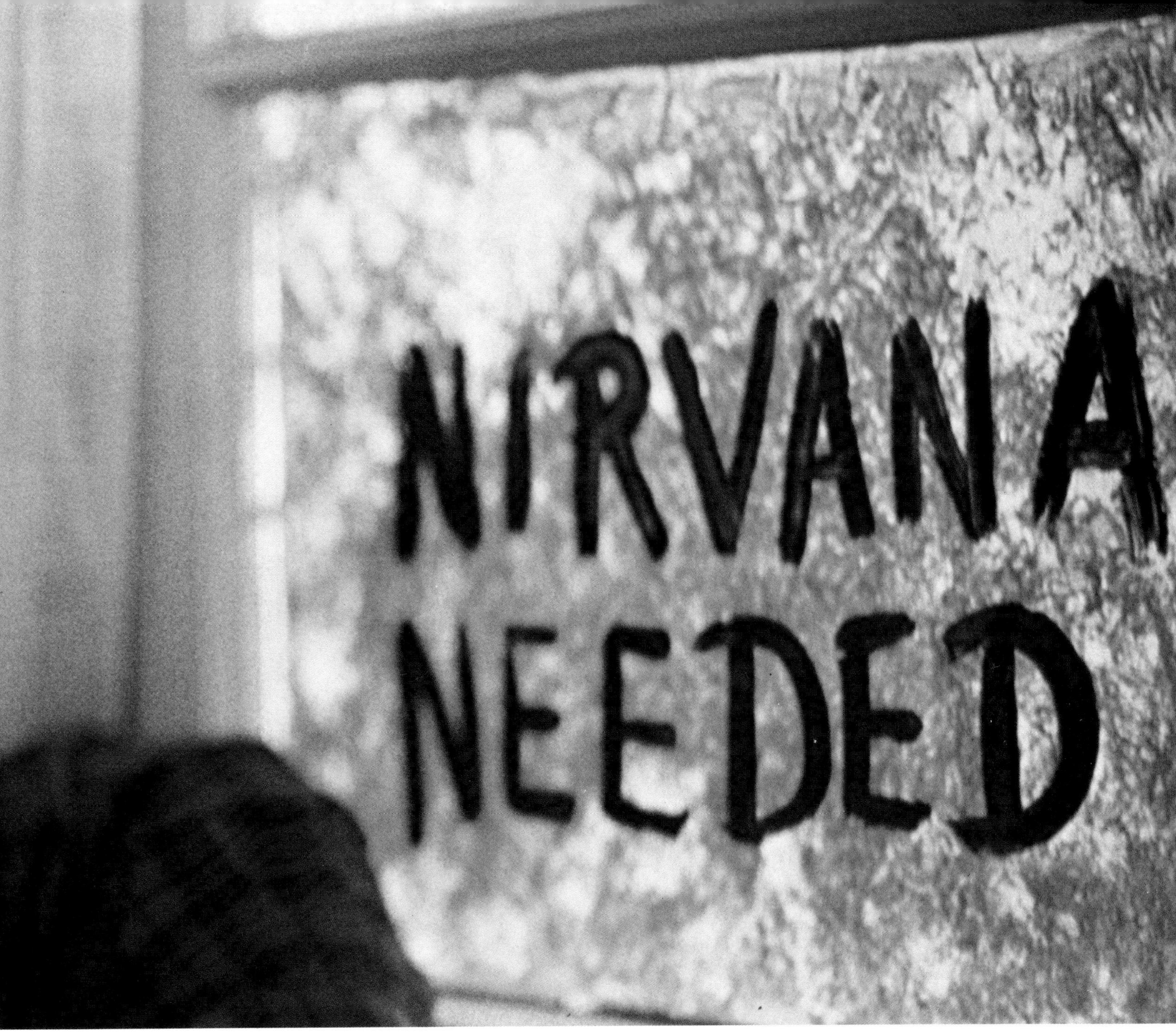

the need for any prescribed way of living. But I can't do it. I'm too well known for one thing; people pester me, and my friends are often my worst enemies. I can't ignore them and I don't even try. Actually you don't have a choice. We *think* we have choices, but your temperament, your character and your previous mode of living – everything that you have done in your life – dictates what you will do, whether you like it or not.

So in a sense I sometimes feel I'm a victim of my own creation. I've created a work now which many people think important, and now I'm paying the penalty. It's backfiring on me in a strange way. People say, "Oh, he must be sitting pretty now. He's got money, that beautiful house, swimming pool, girls always around," and so on. Well, that's an illusion.

It's true my life is never dull, I'll say that. There are so many people coming and going all the time, and I mean by that friends and friends of friends and women passing through that I never suffer from boredom. . . . Sometimes I wish I could be bored, that there would be nothing to do and time would lie heavy on my hands. But I'm accursed, maybe blessed, I don't know which it is, with a mind that is perpetually turning over. The wheels never stop. At night I wake up two or three times to make notes of what I want to do tomorrow. And I don't *want* to do anything tomorrow. But I will do something. I will search for a book I have long wanted to read. My mind never stops.

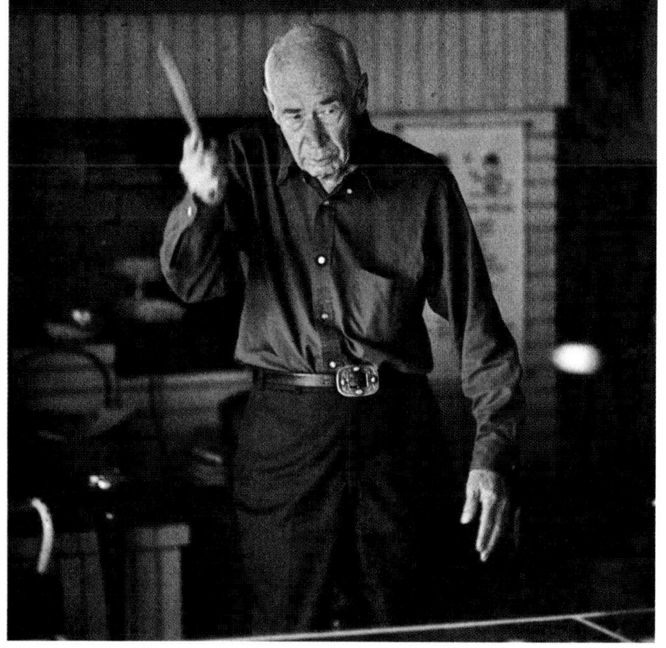

In a way I'm living a great contradiction. Although not too, how should I say it, hurtful to me. I'm living a contradiction in that I'm saying all these things have no importance and yet I make them important. With me there's no trifiing. Everything *I* want to do has to be done. (That's the German in me, which I hate.) And I do it. I carry out these orders, these impulses. I'm always responding, I'm very receptive to everything. A friend talks to me, then leaves, and unwittingly he's dropped a number of things into my noodle. After he leaves I make notes – what did he say now about this or that? – find out more about it! Do you see? It's my nature.

I'm fairly comfortable now financially. I could live two years, perhaps, on what I have saved – I mean if my income stopped, if nothing more came in. However, I think I'll always earn some royalties from my books, enough to keep me alive. But I won't be able to live the way I do now. I won't mind that either. This present way of life doesn't really suit me. I've always lived very poorly; I don't care for luxury. I don't like having servants. I did a lot of housekeeping here myself. For a time I kept the whole house myself. I swept the floors, washed the dishes, and cooked the meals. I don't like to do this any more, but I can do it. I got the habit in Paris where I did everything myself. I used to cook some wonderful meals for my friends in a space you'd never believe possible. I don't know how I did it. I still cook for myself now and then.

My ideal day would be, first of all, no interruptions, no telephone calls, no visitors, and no letters to answer that are immediate or important. A day for myself. Well, then I might decide to write some letters of my own accord, which I enjoy doing. I would get up very late; only when I felt like jumping out of bed with vigor and vim. I would have no regard for time. What time of the day it might be – Fuck it! That's one of the things that bothers me most of all – what time is it? Time to eat, time to do this or that – no, I hate that. Let me say that in a good mood I might even write something aside from letters, because there are many things that I would still like to write. I'm not talking about a big book.

But first of all I would have a good swim. And then I would like some time during the day, preferably late afternoon, for a good friend and good ping pong player to drop in so I could spend a couple of hours playing ping pong. I'd swim, I'd have my ping pong. A French meal, if possible. Then I would love to see a good movie, which I seldom do in the evening. If I don't find the movie that I want, I may go to see a Japanese movie, take a chance. Nine times out of ten I enjoy them. But nine times out of ten if I go see a movie that is advertised as a smash hit I walk out after ten or fifteen minutes. I rarely see a first class film. (A wonderful exception recently was Fellini's *Satyricon.*) Finally I'd read. I always read in bed and I always have about six or eight books at the bedside. I go from one to the other.

This is my seventieth year of ping pong playing. I started at the age of ten on the dining room table. The focal point in my home is the ping pong room. I take on players from all over the world. I play a steady, defensive Zen-like game. The importance of this recreation lies in preventing intellectual discussions. No matter how important or glamorous my opponent may be I never let him or her distract me.

At home with two of my favorite Orientals—my wife Hoki and her seductive friend Puko. At one time I had as permanent guests five lovely slant-eyed beauties in my Pacific Palisades home.

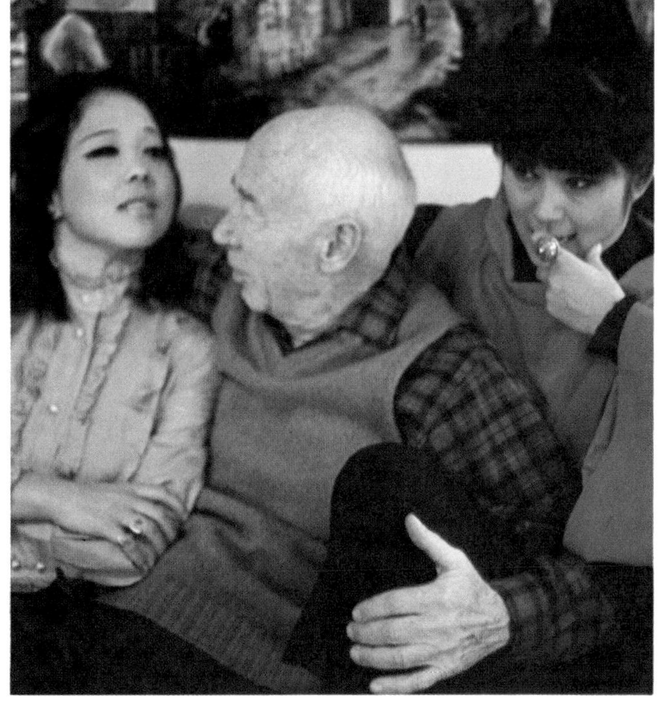

When Hoki-san is on tour in Japan the evenings pass pleasantly in the company of her friend—and mine—Puko. Her right name is Fumiko but Puko, her nickname, seems better to suit her personality. When she enters a room I always feel the warmth of her radiant spirit.

I'm always happy if a woman walks in, and of course they do. I'm going to tell you about all that available cunt. It isn't the all important thing for me to get a lay. I'm much more interested in being able to have a good time with a woman and if it's a matter of going to bed, fine, but if it isn't it's also all right. That's no longer the *sine qua non*, right. I appreciate women around like you would appreciate flowers. They add something to the atmosphere; they make life more interesting. I've always preferred to have women around rather than men. But I'm a good friend and I have a very few close men friends. I make friends easily, but I don't want a lot more friends. My life is loaded with friends, but they have impeded my progress so to speak, more than helped me. That's a cruel way of putting it. It's not exactly what I mean. I'm indebted to my friends for many things, but when it comes to doing what I want it's my friends who get in my way more than my enemies. They make great demands on my time. Don't mistake me. I appreciate friendship. There's no misanthropy in me, and I believe I'm loyal.

Puko is one of my favorite listeners. Here I am telling her an outrageous story about being born with a full set of teeth, and how the first thing I did was to bite the breast that fed me.

Varda

Here I am with two famous old friends—Anaïs Nin and Jean Varda. The occasion is an exhibition of Varda's collages. In the realm of collage Varda is a master, as he is in life.

But because I attract so many people, people sometimes bug me, get in my hair. When I hear the doorbell ring, Jesus! I remember reading about D. H. Lawrence, how he used to hide in the kitchen, anywhere not to be caught. "Don't say I'm home," that's what I say all the time. "Say I've gone on a trip." I don't think it's age that has brought about this attitude, yet it must be a factor. It's a phobia with me, just as the telephone is a phobia, has been all my life, ever since the Western Union job when I had three telephones on my desk and I was trying to talk to three people at the same time. Well, all my life people are coming to see me; they are largely people I don't know, that I didn't invite. That can be good, bad or indifferent, but how can one handle all this? It's a human impossibility. I love to be with my own real friends. Sometimes I open the door to a stranger and he proves to be a wonderful person. But that doesn't mean I want to see him again. Once is enough.

In the beginning of your life you form strong friendships; you help solve each other's problems. Well, I don't have that kind of need any more. It's been a long time since I had that kind of need.

The telephone is my bête noir. To me it's an invention of the devil. I could do without it if I were living alone. Those who are most persistent in ringing through are always the ones you don't want to hear from.

When I look at myself in the mirror I cannot resist the temptation to see how I would look if I really were a clown. As you can see I'm not too bad at it.

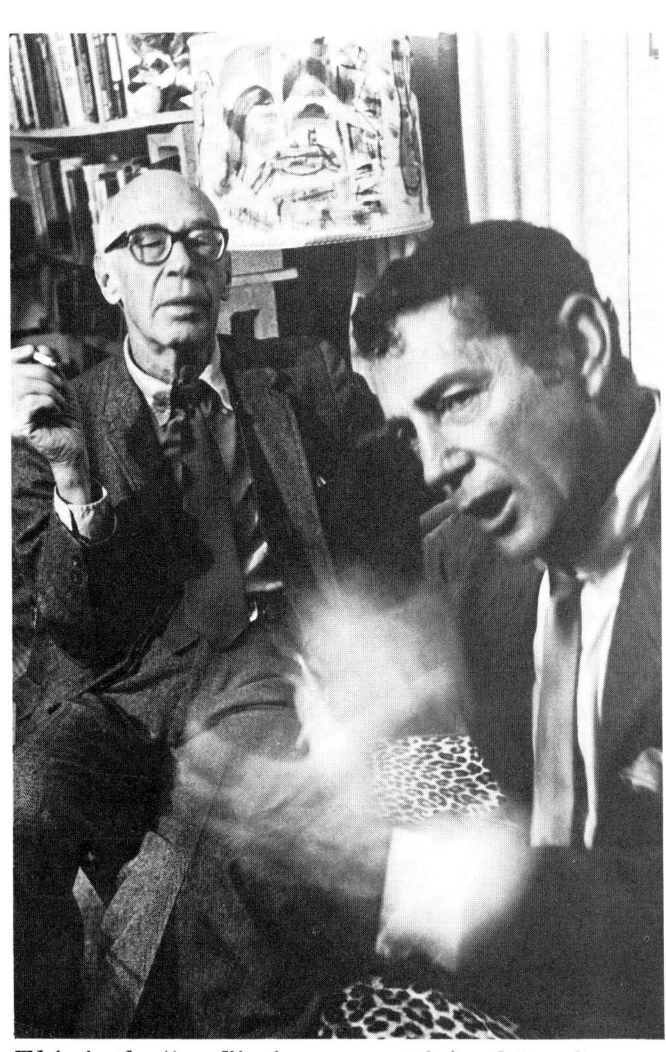

This is the "pad" of my great friend Joe Gray whose walls are decorated with my "failures." I can't imagine a life in Pacific Palisades without the frequent visits of Joe whose talk is always of books, boxing and "unrequited love."

TORO
DIMANCHE

I have one very good friend who I see constantly. He wants nothing from me. His name is Joe Gray. I met Joe one night some ten years ago at a party at Bernie Wolf's home. Bernie is the one who wrote *Really the Blues.* Joe walked in and we got to talking. We were only chatting a few minutes when Joe says, "We come from the same neighborhood in Brooklyn." And I said, "Weren't you a fighter once?" He had that look, you know. We began to talk about boxing and fighters. That endeared him to me. Then he began talking books. He told me all that he was reading, and it was great! Byron I discovered was one of his great favorites. He likes Keats and Shelley, but Byron especially, and he can quote at length from him. When I was going through one of my lovesickness periods – a rather prolonged one – Joe would come to me with little slips of paper with quotes from Byron. "You think you've had it, look what *he* said!"

He's an actor and stunt man – rather famous among Hollywood extras. He's absolutely natural and he doesn't give a shit about anybody. Yet one night, when he was being interviewed, he got literary on me, if you know what I mean, *acting*, of all things. He couldn't help it. I wanted him to be just his natural self, talk his own lingo, which is highly refreshing. He has his own special idiomatic language. He knows how to listen too. He digs what you say, even if it's over his head. One night he invited a girl over whom he had met at the studio. I think she was a Nisei. He told me she was cute. I never can depend on his judgment though. He looks first at a woman's legs – he loves legs. Then he looks at the breasts. They must have big breasts. I suspect he looks at the face last.

Joe Gray collects women—only good looking ones—like other people collect coins or paintings. And he is most generous in passing them on to his friends, especially yours truly.

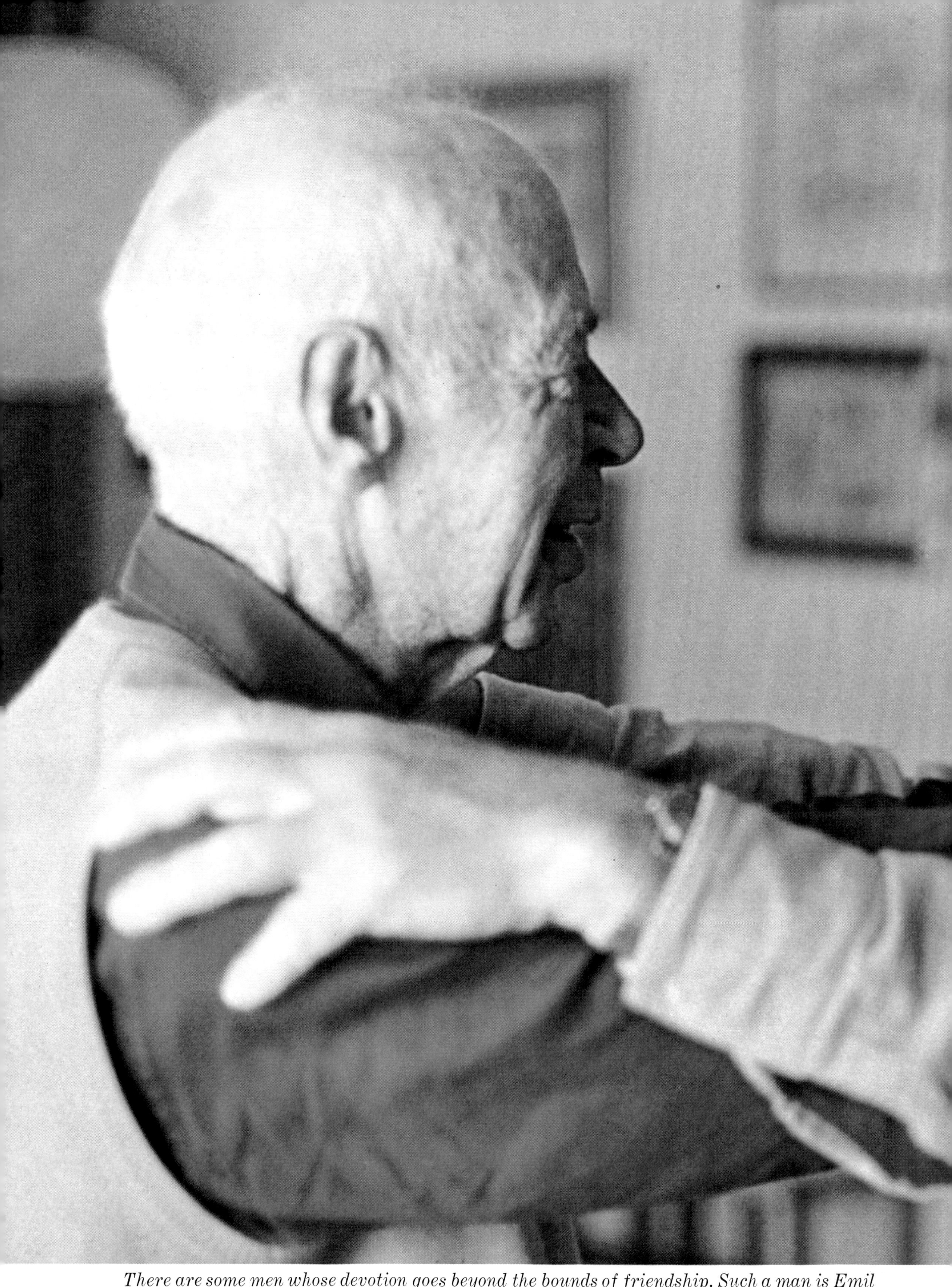

There are some men whose devotion goes beyond the bounds of friendship. Such a man is Emil

White. For 25 years I've known that I could depend on Emil for anything—and I mean anything.

Recently, in the last year or so, I've become interested in music again, and particularly the piano which I used to play years ago. I had the great good fortune to make friends with Jakob Gimpel, the concert pianist. Now I go twice a month to his home to attend his master class. I must say that that is one of the greatest inspirations in recent years – to attend that class. It opens up all sorts of new directions to me. You see, most of his pupils are very accomplished pianists. Each one plays whatever has been agreed on beforehand. After they have played their piece through he makes them go through it again, stopping and correcting them, showing them precisely what's wrong and showing them what they lack in interpretation. I must stress that word *interpretation* – for this is what gives me such a delight. Concerning everything in life that word is one of the biggest words I know – *interpretation*. Consider the field of astrology. There are astrologers and astrologers. The only ones who are worthwhile are those that have the gift of interpretation. Anyone can learn to set up a chart, but it is something else to give a good interpretation of a man's character and destiny. Well, it's the same in music, in criticism, in writing, in painting. I learn a little more about the art of interpretation every time I go to this master class.

I never play the piano seriously any more. Now and then I sit down and clown it – imitate some pianist's histrionic style, make believe I am playing. Of course I hit all the wrong notes. I never attempt to play seriously because it involves too much work. As a pianist, I lacked that one important thing, talent. That's why I gave it up. I can't improvise and I can't interpret. It means nothing to me to be able to sit down and play a Beethoven sonata. Could I ever learn to play it like Mr. Gimpel or his pupils? Never, never in my life. Could I learn to play it fairly well? Possibly. If you can't do these things well there is no fun in it. My ear is too well trained to be satisfied with a mediocre performance.

Everything involves time and discipline. You must practice regularly or you lose out. You have to be it and do it every day; that is one of the reasons why a man like Picasso is so marvelous. He never loses his touch because he is constantly at it. He doesn't even have to think any more. It's right there in his fingers. He picks up the brush, and the brush tells him what to do, or so I imagine.

When Gimpel, the master, interrupts a pupil's performance it is often to emphasize the extraordinary range of control which the proper use of the fingers can give. Here he has gone to the piano to demonstrate his point.

Music has always been an important thing in my life. Through my marriage to Hoki, a singer and pianist, it became more so. One of our permanent guests aspires to be an opera singer. We have Madame Butterfly for breakfast, lunch and dinner.

When my daughter Val was a little girl we would sit on the piano bench and play at playing the piano together. In this picture, taken when she recently visited me, we are doing our old piano trick.

Once I did play the piano. Now I play with it. I come up with a lot of great sounds which could never be mistaken for music. Some people get the impression that I am an avant garde pianist.

Now there must be something perverse about me. What I mean is that I want to be the opposite of what I am, and yet to be very frank and honest with you, I am very happy just as I am. I wouldn't want to change. There it is – a frightful contradiction. I admit it shamelessly. I stress this matter of *being* versus *doing* because it's not just my conflict, it's the conflict of the modern world. We are at the stage now where we can look upon our activity, not our creation, but our activity, and say it stinks. It is the ruination of our world. This busy bee activity, this senseless activity–that's what I'm against.

I must add one other thing. I must tell you that there is always a part of my life that I keep secret – even from my closest friends. This secret part I never write about, and it's a very important part of me. (There is one little section of one's life which is being continually reduced in size and this remote part, this area

This is Lisa Lu, one of the most respected actresses of the Chinese theater. Knowing her has opened new vistas in my life.

of the mind, may be the very important thing that sustains us, that permits you to go through what you do go through in life.)

I am a man who's constantly falling in love. People say I am an incurable romantic. Perhaps I am. In any case I'm grateful to the powers that be that I am that way. It's brought me sorrow *and* joy; I wouldn't want it any other way. People work better, create better, when they are in love. For it's true that if you are creative there is a lot of work involved. I often think of the Old Testament–and how God created the world in six days and then He found it good and He stopped. Supposedly He was satisfied with his creation.

But to me that is not an accurate picture of creation, because creation goes on continually; once you have begun you are part and parcel of your own creation and you cannot stop. All of us who have some awareness and some intelligence know that we have to play a role in life. I don't say we *elect* our role; maybe we were forced into it. But we do find ourselves playing a role. People often say, "Oh I can do this, or I could do that," but it's not true. There is no choice. You are what you are and you will be what you are. But this business of having a role to play, whether it's a humble one or a big one, doesn't matter; it gives traction to the ego, gives meaning to your life. You are fulfilled if you play your role to the best of your ability. The tragedy of our world is that people are not aware of their role, have no consciousness of it. They are to be pitied.

At some time everyone who has interviewed me has asked me how I happened to become a writer. I have given an answer that is part true, but the other part I don't know. I explain that I tried everything else and I was a failure, why not try writing? That's not a complete answer, and yet there is truth in it. The truth is I was afraid to become a writer. I didn't think I had the ability – it was too big a thing. Who was I to say *I am a writer?* I meant

writer with a capital W – a writer like Dostoevsky, Joyce, Lawrence and so on. So I put it behind me.

Every day men are squelching their instincts, their desires, their impulses, their intuitions. One has to get out of the fucking machine he is trapped in and do what he wants to do. But we say no, I have a wife and children, I better not think of it. That is how we commit suicide every day. It would be better if a man did what he liked to do and failed than to become a successful nobody. Isn't that so?

I feel that a hunted, perilous and fear-ridden life is preferable to that of the salesman with his briefcase. It's *your* life, *your* misery, your own misfortune. Thus you're all of a piece. Whatever happens, good or bad, *you* are taking it, not some double. A salesman is a man with a split personality. One side of him is a husband, a father, a protector of a family; the other side is a man who's a slave, who knuckles down and says yes to his boss and does all manner of things that he doesn't believe in. But when you're stripped and have to beg for help, you're nothing but yourself; you're naked, exposed and vulnerable. You feel that you're carrying your own self all the time. It's true that there are two kinds of servitude. You can't get away from it; they're both terrible and ugly. But in doing what you like you still have a sense of freedom even if it's a freedom to starve and suffer.

Perhaps there's a profound truth here – after all, in the highest sense, life is *servitude.* But there is voluntary servitude and involuntary servitude. Voluntary servitude takes in the truly great figures. I don't mean to include myself when I say that. I'm speaking of much greater figures, like St. Francis, for instance. He elected to dedicate himself to a life of service to humanity and underwent all manner of humiliation and sacrifice willingly, even gladly.

I'm intrigued very much with the thought that I too may be what is called a split personality. Several times recently my palm has been read and they always discover that the heart and head lines run together. This is unusual, supposedly. What does it mean? I don't know. I thought at first it meant conflict. But it's more like thinking and feeling. To the person who thinks with his head life is a comedy. To those who think with their feelings, or work through their feelings, it's a tragedy. I think there is a lot of that in me. I always have this feeling of being split. I can see two ways often. I am not a logical thinker. My feelings dictate my thinking a great deal. When expressing it in writing I usually try to avoid saying whether I'm an optimist or pessimist. I'd like to believe there's something beyond the opposites. I think that's the real viewpoint.

One of the more spectacular beauties who used to visit me occasionally was the Israeli actress Ziva Rodann. We indulged in a lot of innocent horseplay.

The "world" is usually used by way of comparison with something else. Do you know what I mean when I say that a man is *of* the world or *in* the world or *not* of it? In that sense then the world comes to represent something that man fights, struggles against. He wants to be in it but not of it. He wants to be above it. However, I do believe that the only way you can prove you are not of it is by entering into it fully. You cannot evade anything that is of this world. You must accept everything that belongs to this world and then show that there is something more.

That doesn't mean that you shouldn't have standards of acceptance or rejection. You should not fall prey, you should not fall into the trap which the world presents. You should be able to enter it, partake of it, understand it, and yet know that what is moving and directing you, guiding you through life, is not altogether represented by the world in which one lives, that there are other things, invisible, inscrutable, intangible, which the concept of "world" does not include or embrace.

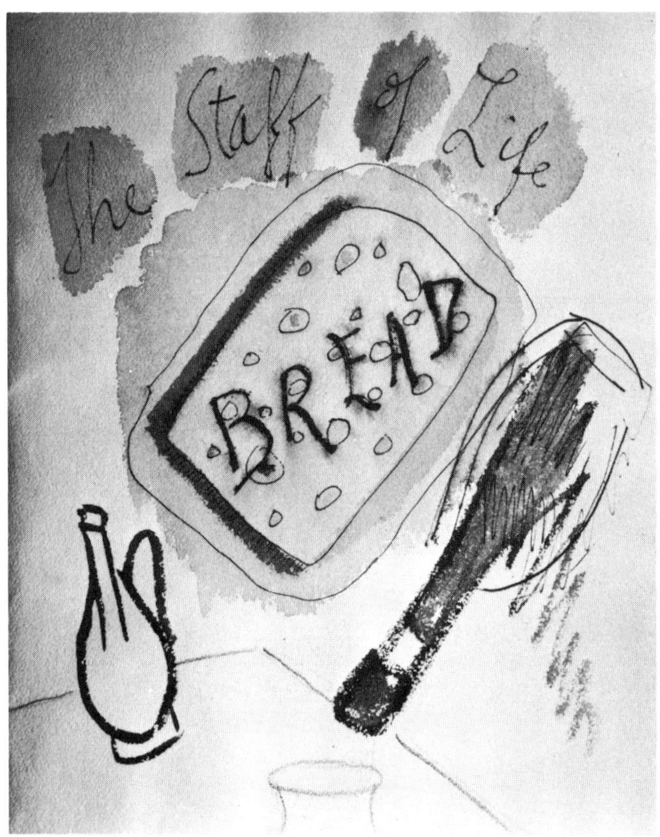

I'm a religious man but not a religionist. Let's put it very simply. When we say that "man does not live by bread alone," that's a symbolic statement tersely put. What it means is that it isn't his success in the struggle for life – his getting bread, getting security, protecting wife and children – that sustains and supports him. It's something you can't put your finger on, it's spirit. You can't name it, can't define it. It's greater than everything else; it includes everything.

I think I sense it when I come in contact with it. I think you're aware of it when you talk to people. There are those of poor spirit and those of great spirit. None are without it, but the flame flickers pretty low in some cases. The majority of people seem to be nothing but a little flickering flame. You know that when you match them against an individual who is all fire, all radiance. Those in whom the flame of the spirit runs high are extraordinary examples of human beings.

Most of us are just folks. That's true, but yet we don't get very far nourishing that idea. This is something I'm always against – to regard people as just "folks." It's nice and folksy to talk that way and it means let's be warm and neighborly and *simpatico*. O.K. Sometimes, and I think even saintly men have the desire and act on it too, sometimes it's necessary to goad people; you have to give them a nudge, a poke, a push. You have to jab them to awaken them. One does it out of kindness in order to make them aware of themselves, of their potentialities. Most of us are living far below our potential.

When we say "just folks" we mean all those who are living below the horizon line, who haven't come up. They're there like a soft cushion on which we're all comfortably floating. It's true these "folks" are the ones who support us. It's they who are doing the work of the world. But even they could do other work, do bigger work. I don't think what is called the work of the world, this everyday work that is glorified, is really so important. It would be much much better if people were told to be lazy, shirk their jobs, be idlers, enjoy, relax, not care, not worry. I think we'd get all that work done some other way. It's pretty much the same – daily work and dirty work.

Jesus said, "consider the lilies of the field, how they grow; they toil not, neither do they spin." The thought behind it is that we are creating this work, not because it has to be done but because we are busybodies and do not know how to swim on the stream of life. We prefer a kind of senseless insect activity to a genuine activity which may often be no activity, plain inaction. I don't say to be quiet, to do nothing. But I say what we do should have sense, should have meaning. And the greater part of what we do every day has damn little meaning.

I'm going to say something that sounds like the very opposite of what I just said, and very often the truth has this paradoxical quality. You can see it as two opposing things making one. What I mean is that a man who fully enters into the life we have today and who does it consciously and deliberately enjoys what he's doing. He is almost as free as the man who cuts adrift from it. When you fully accept something, you are no longer victimized by it. But those are rare men.

Many times I look at ordinary people, common, humble people, and I envy them. I admire them. They do not question as we are questioning one another now or questioning

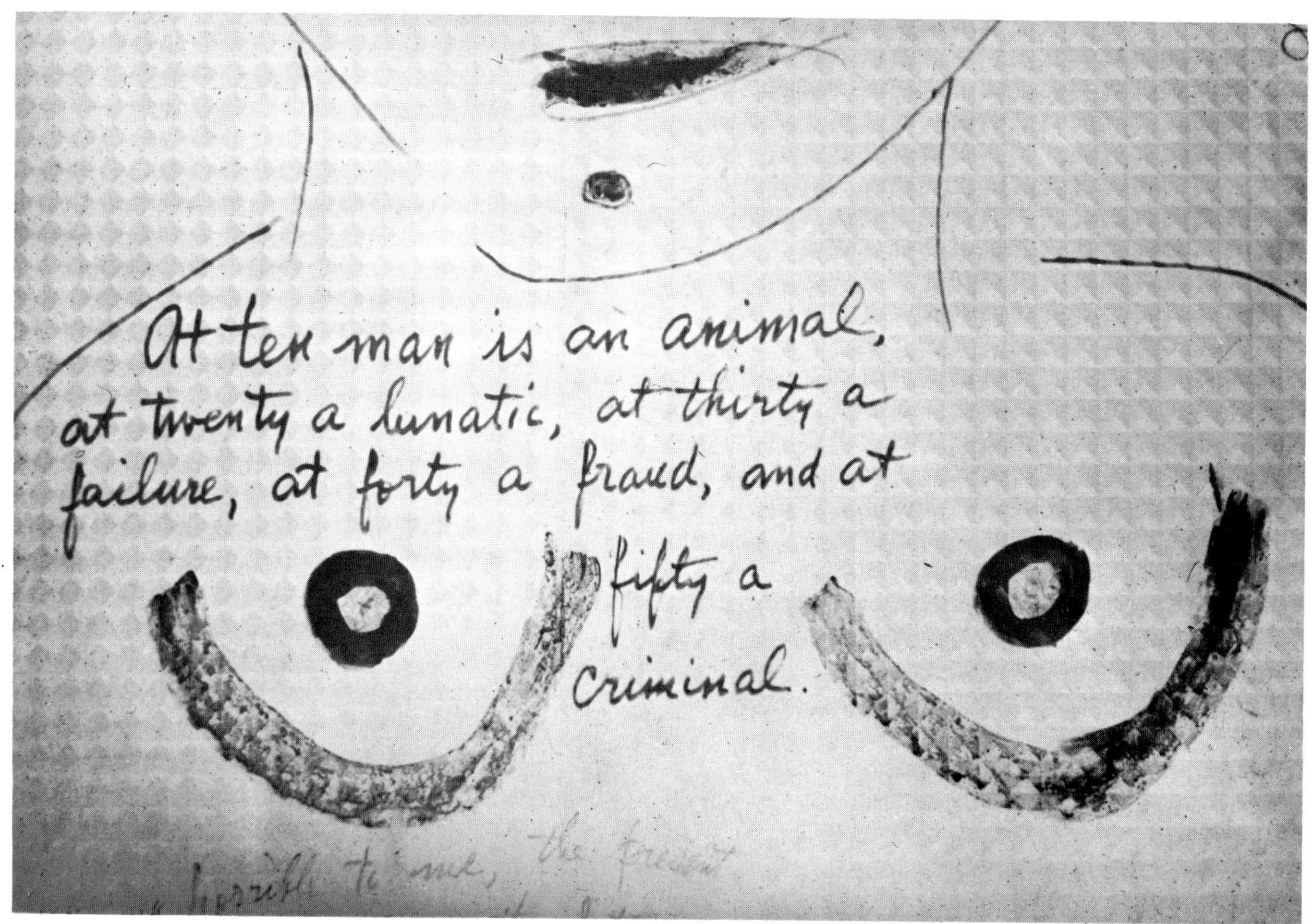

One of many quotations on the walls of my studio. This one by a famous Japanese author who might prefer to remain unidentified. I am impressed by the truth of his words.

the world or its ways. They have never raised their voice this way. They've taken what has been offered them to do and they've done it. In a way there's something beautiful and noble about that. They are simple souls. They are souls even if they do not express it in terms of faith in a religious way. Really they are moving like religious figures. They've accepted their lot. Now, what we know about the neurotic is that he's a paralyzed man. He can't act, he can't move, he can't write or paint or whatever it is that he wishes to do. He's always thinking, thinking in terms of the future or the past, thinking in terms of perfection. This is his great sin, so to speak. Take, for example, the Surrealists. Through writing automatically they discovered that one experiences a great release the moment one stops thinking and forgets the importance of what he's doing and just lets "it" come out. "It" knows what it's doing.

So often in writing I found it difficult to begin. But I began. I began with anything that came to mind — sheer nonsense usually. After a page or two, I found myself in the groove. It doesn't matter where you start from, you always come back to what you are. You can't get away from what you are. Take men like Flaubert, Balzac, Henry James, who are considered rather objective writers. They didn't write in the first person. They created types, imagined characters. Always something outside themselves. Nevertheless, you can always see Henry James, you can always see Balzac, in what they wrote. Turgenev versus Dostoevsky for example. Dostoevsky was delivering himself all the time. Turgenev was the polished stylist, the academician. But Turgenev couldn't get away from himself either. You recognize him in every line. It doesn't matter how you approach a thing, you'll always come back to your own self and your own obsessive themes. Dali, by the way, spoke about the obsessive mania in the artist as though to say an artist is really no good unless he is possessed and obsessed. And certainly Dostoevsky was a possessed man. Dali strikes me more as an obsessed man. They are both examples of men who were in the grip of something bigger than themselves.

Other artists try to avoid this. By "others" I mean those whom the world looks upon more favorably, as more finished, more accomplished artists. A great novelist like Tolstoy, for example, would be regarded in this way. On the other hand, I give you Dickens. A totally opposite sort of individual. Who moved the world more? I would say Dickens. I really think Dickens moved the world more than Tolstoy. I think that Dickens is going to outlast Tolstoy. He struck a deeper human level. And, by the way, let's inject another note, he was also a great humorist. That is his great, great quality. He made us laugh at ourselves.

I think it was Baudelaire who said, "Be drunken always." But what does that mean? Be always ecstatic! Be always filled with a divine intoxication! That was the meaning of it. It wasn't drunkenness in the brutal sense. And who celebrated that more in his writing than Rabelais? I have a wonderful passage in one of my books in which I quote Arthur Machen, the Welsh writer. He talks about the obscenity of Rabelais, talks about the long obscene word lists that Rabelais reels off. He says something to the effect, "Observe that this is no ordinary cataloguing. This is something abnormal. This is something super-normal, supercharged; it has a meaning beyond all this."

You couldn't find two societies in the Western world more different than that of New York of 1850 and Paris of 1850 and yet Baudelaire found a link in the works and character of Edgar Allen Poe. In a sense they were both outcasts. Poe was a somewhat disreputable figure. Baudelaire even more so. He made himself such. He spat on society. We have this all the time, these correspondences between seemingly unlike places, unlike men.

In my book on Rimbaud there is a coda at the end which is a sort of Surrealist bit. I went through all manner of books looking for dates and names and titles in order to write those two or three pages. What I tried to show is that, as the 19th Century drew to a close, the artists who were prominent in that century were all tragic figures. The 19th Century, as you know, was a century of material progress, so-called enlightenment, rationalism, etc. Yet the artists of that period were against these things. They were all crucified. Many met early deaths, horrible deaths. Nietzsche ends up in the asylum. Van Gogh and Rimbaud both die within a year of each other at the age of 34. It's a whole catalog of disaster. Yet all these men were filled with a vision of something better to come.

Most bathrooms are the dullest room in the house. Not so at the Miller manse. This is a section of the montage covering the walls. I often find my visitors spending more than the allotted time in the bathroom. There is everything on the walls—from fakirs and sages to houris and whores. I too enjoy sitting here and contemplating my handiwork.

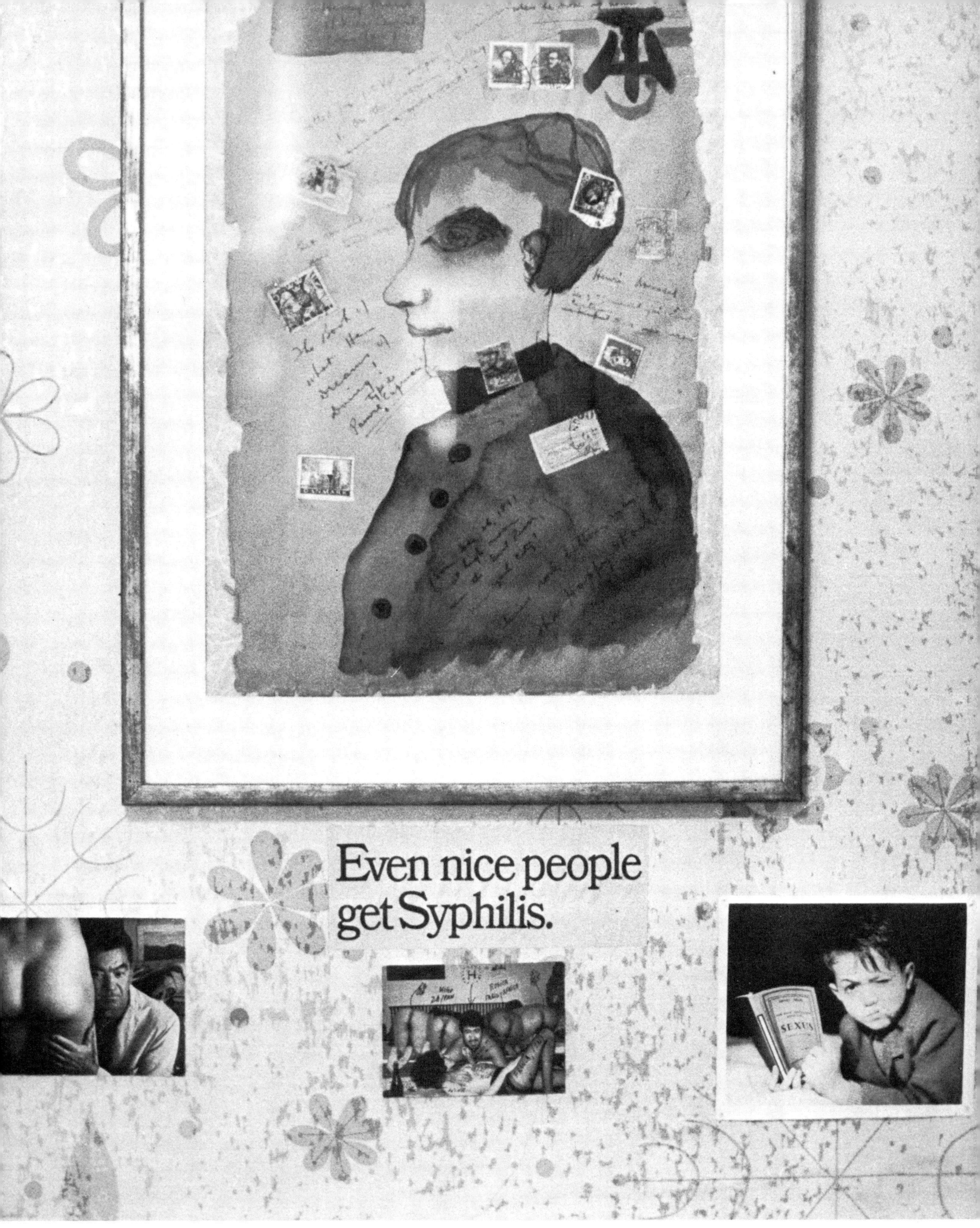

This is the montage directly above the toilet bowl in my private bathroom. Because of the different positions assumed by men and women in relieving the bladder, men have a greater opportunity to observe this montage.

I speak about the tortured spirits because it was the tortured spirits who reflected "spirit." It was the spirit that was being tortured in that century. The afflicted ones are so because they try to preserve what is vital to us. Take Blake. He began in the 18th and moved into the 19th. He was a great figure, a prophetic figure, an enigmatic one. Then you have Nietzsche. Then a mad man like Strindberg. What revolt! What a castigation of society! These figures reveal the modern world falling apart. Its dilemmas are petty dilemmas. Men like Blake, Ibsen, Nietzsche – they represent in their work modern man's peculiar tragedy. They previsioned it. They foresaw what was happening to the world and to man. They got to the real crux of man's problems.

Man in the 19th Century began to feel a loneliness such as he'd never felt before, at least as I read history. He's been feeling it for a century now and he's getting more and more lonely, more and more atomized. He's being blown to smithereens. He's in a world where he has no bearings. He's on his own as he's never been before, because in the past he had tradition and convention. There's nothing on the horizon today: no great leaders, no Moses who might lead us out of the wilderness. Now it is up to man to save himself. He can't look to anyone for help. That's the desperate and the hopeful quality about this modern age. Man has to recognize himself as something more than a human being or he'll perish.

It's been said that we will never have another saviour. There have been enough saviours. They all have shown man the way. Now man must save himself. Ultimately this is a good thing. Man's position now is tragic in the sense that it's profoundly weighted with good and bad. There's a risk, a challenge. Live or perish. Live up to your maximum! The religious history of the world has been that of man living with crutches. Now we're throwing those crutches away. Now we have the choice of accepting or rejecting God. It's not in the hereafter that things may be realized, but now.

In Western thought it's always good or bad. But in Hindu metaphysics they arrive at a point beyond that, and that's the only solution – to transcend conflicts, not to look upon one thing, one idea, as right and the other wrong. You have to have a vision that embraces the two. It's almost a God-like attitude, since God is supposed to look upon man and events impartially. You're dead tomorrow; this or that happens. God doesn't worry about you. They say He looks after the sparrow. To me that's all a lot of shit. As far as we know, God has never taken care of anybody. We've taken care of ourselves and fucked ourselves into the bargain. So when we talk of schizophrenia, I don't think that now we're in a bad period and in some distant period it will be the opposite. I'm not thinking that way at all. I'm thinking the only solution for *homo sapiens* is to die out. Another kind of human being has to come into existence. And he has to have a different consciousness. He won't have these problems of ours. He'll have others. He won't have what I call miserable, petty problems. The lowest problems to me are hunger, war, injustice. These are problems we should have solved eons ago. Any intelligent, sensitive man is above all that. These are not problems to him any more.

You take a man like Krishnamurti whom I was listening to again the other night. Someone had asked him about food for India and he replied that, although it might help a few, the problem was bigger than that. He's one of the few in this world who's not saying think this way, think that way. He says, "Open your eyes, expand your mind!" He's not saying go to this or that church or believe in this or that idea. He says that at bottom all religions

This unknown Chinese sage has played an important role in my reflective life. His face greets me and inspires me when I awake each morning. This photo of me regarding him was taken by Red Skelton when visiting me at Big Sur.

are alike. They offer an escape, not a solution.

I've noticed that there is more Eastern influence in writing and philosophy than ever before. I was interested in Chinese philosophy when I was eighteen, and later Hindu philosophy, but when I speak of Krishnamurti, there's a man who rules it all out. I too believe philosophy never did anybody any good. Metaphysics is another matter. These are games that man plays. He has a mind; he has to use it. This affords entertainment but no more than that. Man doesn't live by it. Krishnamurti was asked about death. He says, "Well, who knows about that?" That's so true. Nobody knows about it. Why bother about it? The main thing is not to fear. In a way the scientists are free of that. They're dealing with the unknown too but they're not worried like religious people are. They have problems they set themselves and their problems are about unknown things. But they go to work detachedly. Yet I do believe man should always have the problem of life and death before him. I don't like the idea of having problems that

are always solvable. You should really take it all to heart and be torn apart until your eyes are opened. Then these problems disappear, they sink below the level of consciousness.

In one sense it's very different to be a writer now than when I was writing in Paris. Let's say that today the writer gets money easier, he gets published more quickly. But what kind of publishers and what kind of writing? They're not taking the best writing. It's no solution for the truly creative ones. They always have difficulty because they're always in advance of their age. They're always going to be crucified until we bring about a totally different kind of society, one in which the artist is recognized for what he truly is, a leader and a healer. I don't see that coming in the near future.

People have said to me that I knew that kind of life when I was living in Paris because I was so broke. But I can't say that. After all, a bohemian is not a down and outer. I was down and out by choice, which is a different thing. It had almost a romantic quality.

I'm in love with a saying I found some time ago and now I have found it again in a book by Alan Watts. It's by Gautama the Buddha and it goes like this: "I obtained not the least thing from complete unexcelled awakening and for that very reason it is called complete unexcelled awakening."

My hours haven't improved. I remember in Paris waking up late, but here I can't seem to get on the right level. Now I'm beginning to enjoy my midnight hours. After the TV and the comedians I can read the most profound books, books that require all my concentration. I'm at my best at noon and that's the hour I was born. In astrology they say that's your best time, the hour you were born, and it was so for many years with me. I remember it because I would be writing at full speed about noontime. It was then, just then, that my wife would call and say lunch is ready. It was hard to stop.

I am a film addict and a book addict too, but they are not equal in effect. The film satisfies something in me which books don't. The film satisfies the eye, for one thing. I think first of all that one of the big differences between the two is that a film doesn't stay with you as a book does. A book is real meat and substance, and you live with it and it nourishes you. A film, if it's a good one, is something which gives you a few wonderful moments and then fades away. Certainly you may recall certain things, but it doesn't hang with you for days on end, not even the best film, whereas a book you can't shake off. You live it over and over again for days and weeks, and it comes back to you again and again. It leaves a permanent impression upon you if it is a good book. Films don't do that to me. What I do notice about films is that certain characters become imbedded in the back of your head. You can bring them to life over and over again. With a book you never know how a certain character ever looked. You have to imagine him.

The motion picture image is a very, very strong one. It is more satisfying, to me, than the theatre. I used to go to the theatre a great deal. Today I hardly ever go. A moderately good play I can't stand. A poor film I can sometimes sit through because something is going on; indeed many things are going on at once. It isn't the story that holds me. There is color and movement. Action. There are also types I recognize, who are very close to me. Some are attractive, others horrible but memorable. You're observing living people and they become more real, more close to you in some ways, than characters in a book. I can think back to films I saw thirty or forty years ago and I still remember certain individuals and I can summon them to mind and eye. The

characters in a book I never really visualize. They leave some sort of image, but it is blurred or vague.

I think the period of printing and reading must soon come to an end and must be replaced by something else. Yet, since I am a writer and words mean so much to me, it is difficult to imagine what the substitute will be. You get something in books that no film can ever give: the associations which words conjure up, ideas that beg to be developed, and so on. These things can never be expressed in films. The film is too real, too concrete. What we love about books is elaboration, fantasy, complexity, for which the film has no time. The film has to be explicit. What we crave is a kind of fuzziness, the aura of the intangible. The film deals with tangibles. It may suggest the other, but not very well, in my opinion. But I will say that we could very well dispense with the bulk of books that are being published—they have no importance, they give us nothing. That may be true of most films as well, but if one had to choose I would say go to see a good film rather than waste your time on most contemporary literature.

The tragedy of the film has been that it derives mostly from literature. This is what has crippled the film. I say we have not yet developed the film media and all of its possibilities as we should have. The film is still in embryo, in my opinion. I would say—throw away the script. Don't have a script. I would say put the actors, director, and cameramen together, give them a rough idea of what's to happen, and then begin to work, to improvise, to build the story as you go along, *if there must be a story*. Of course there doesn't have to be a story. That's exactly what I'm driving at. The film can be greater if it has perfect freedom—when it permits fantasy, reverie, dreams to enter, and all manner of disconnected things. There does not always have to be a reason for things to happen. I admit it is a debatable thing whether there should be any plot. I am on the side of the least form possible, in films as well as in literature. But I know that form is an important element in the making of a film. I realize that more and more.

Just recently I saw Fellini's *Satyricon*. I've also watched him being interviewed a couple of times. His words are golden to me. He talks the language of a creative individual. To the average audience the *Satyricon* comes as a shock. They say, "What is he aiming at?" "What is he saying?" "What is it all about?" I say don't ask me. I only know that I enjoyed every minute of it. I don't give a shit about what it means. What I saw was marvelous. Everything was wonderful—and why can't we just have that, a series of marvelous, interesting shots that in themselves are gripping. It was more than that, of course. It's also possible to have a great story, but maybe that's asking for too much. How many great stories are there, how many great novels are there, how many great paintings are there? And how many great films have we had thus far?

We are now in an advanced stage of ripeness. If we are honest with ourselves we must admit that when we go into a museum we find very few great paintings which are still of absorbing interest to us. Ninety percent of them are so much shit. This pious preservation of great works of art may have been important in the past, but not today. I say—how do these things affect you now? Have you any relation with them today? It's like these old films, some of them were great in their day—show them today and you have to say—what sort of idiot was I ever to have enjoyed that kind of film?

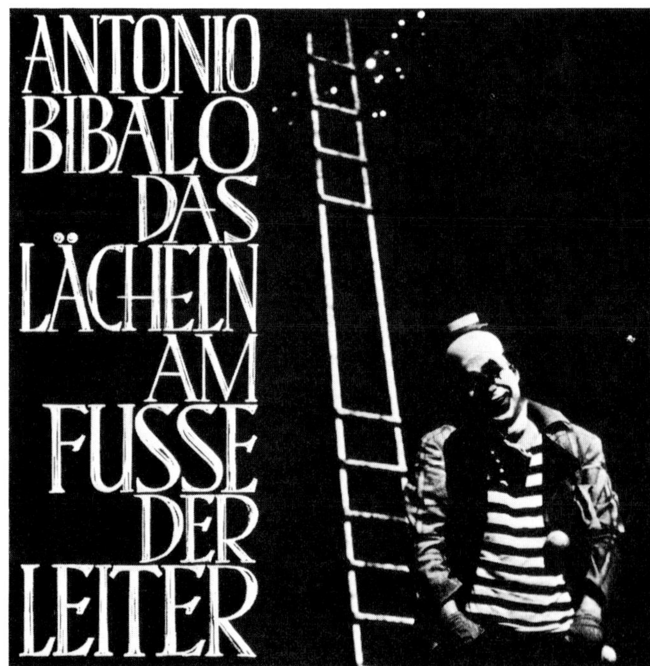

Program from the premiere of the opera based on "The Smile at the Foot of the Ladder" given at the Staatsoper *in Hamburg in 1965. The composer was an Italian named Antonio Bibalo whom I met in Denmark. The opera was later given in Marseilles and in Trieste in French and Italian.*

I struggled in the begin-
ning. I said I was
going to write the truth,
so help me God. And
I thought I was. I
found I couldn't. No-
body can write the
absolute truth.

WRITING

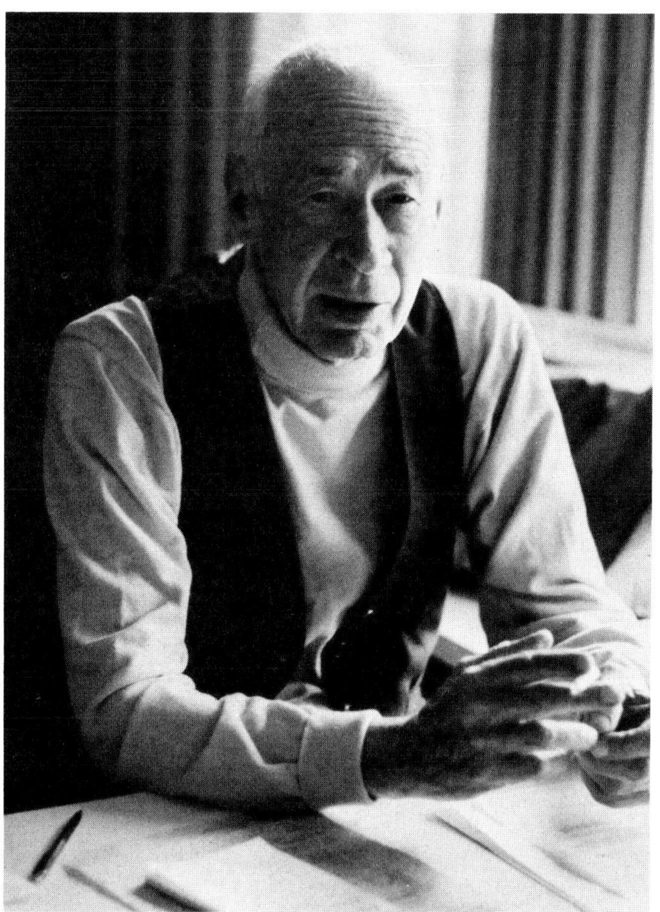

I'm one of those writers who can only write years after the event. Most of my stuff has come out of me twenty years later. One or two books might have been written at the moment, such as the *Tropic of Cancer*, and the *Colossus of Maroussi*. But most of the time I go back. I told you once that I, staying up all night, had made notes in one single stretch of about 12 or 14 hours. That one notebook was the basis of all my autobiographical works. However, when I sit down to write—I'm speaking now of the major works—I only glance briefly at the notes.

With me it's mostly a matter of being tuned up, or tuned in, of being in form mentally and spiritually. Writing, when it does come out, should come out like water from the faucet. The longer I keep this material in me the more gem-like it becomes. It's the result of compression.

When do you begin? How do you start? Most people get frustrated just looking at the blank page. Everybody does. It's the same as looking at a blank canvas. I found a trick that the surrealists discovered, and that was to simply write whatever came to mind—nonsense, no commas, no periods, no sequence of any kind, until what you wanted to say began to come forth. Then you eliminate all the preliminary garbage. I carry on until I grow tired or until I've exhausted what I want to say. But I never let my brain reach the point of exhaustion. I learned a lesson once. I wrote 45 pages one day and then collapsed. So I always try to keep fresh. It's as with a reservoir—you never drain it—it takes too long to fill it up again. Hemingway said that, I think, but Hemingway was another one who slaved over his manuscripts and, in my mind, he did not accomplish too much. I skim off the surplus, as it were, and the next day I have something left over to go on with. That, in general, has been my method of writing. Of course, I get sidetracked very often. I think I'm going to write about a certain thing and suddenly another theme will hit me and I'll go along with it. But the main thing is to keep the stream alive and flowing. Keep the flow—that's the primary thought in my head.

I don't think like other writers. The way I go at it is certainly far different from a movie writer doing a script. He has to think of many, many different things to get it right on the head. I don't care if I miss the target or not. I'm writing, that's the important thing. It's not *what* I have written, it's the writing itself. Because that's my life, writing. The pure act itself is what is most important. *What* I say is not so important. Often it's foolish, nonsensical, contradictory—that doesn't bother me at all. Did I enjoy it? Did I reveal what was in me? That's the thing. And, of course, I don't

Property of
Henry V. Miller
4, Ave. Anatole France
Clichy (Seine) - France

"Tropic of ~~Capricorn~~ Cancer"

by

Anonymous

know what's in me. That's the really important thing. The difference between me and other writers is that they struggle to get down what they've got up here in the head. I struggle to get out what's below, in the solar plexus, in the nether regions.

My friend in Paris, Alfred Perlès, had his own unique method. He would put his watch on the desk and say, "I'm going to write for forty-five minutes." When forty-five minutes passed, he'd stop, even if it were the middle of a sentence. He was finished for the day. I have done this too, stopped in the middle of a paragraph. Now that would annoy many writers because they'd think, "How will I recapture this thought tomorrow?" I never worry about it because I think that nothing is lost. It's only a matter of finding the clue once again. Maybe you don't begin at that paragraph, maybe you begin somewhere else, but eventually, if that was in the back of your head, it will pop out during the course of the writing. And if not that day, then the next day. And if not then, then in the middle of the night. I never worry about things getting lost. Nothing is lost forever, least of all thoughts.

Proust made a point of the fact that in reliving something in memory he was experiencing it even more vividly than when he had actually gone through it. I find that very true. I don't know why it is but perhaps it's because you're extremely conscious and highly aware, very alert, attuned, when writing. You taste more strongly, you feel more strongly about everything. You may, of course, be lying a bit. Though you're recapturing that moment you're also doing things with it. It's yours to deal with, and the point is not so much that it has to be exactly what happened but that it must exude the ambiance, the aura, of that event. I would say it's almost impossible to reproduce a thing absolutely, but certainly you can give the effect of reliving it.

I get a sensual enjoyment out of reliving an experience—maybe even an increased enjoyment. The experience seems heightened. There's a double play going on. The first time you do something, you're not conscious of it, as it were. You don't look at yourself in the mirror. Then, when you are writing, it's just like looking in a mirror and watching yourself doing it all over again. You're leaning over your own self. While you're writing, you're bending over, watching yourself in the act. And you *know* you're performing this time. That's the difference beween the conscious and the unconscious action. I said before that I think by reliving an experience, the enjoyment, the sensual enjoyment, is heightened. That's because when you lived the situation originally there were no words accompanying it. You weren't saying to yourself, "Oh, how wonderful the fog is, the touch of it on my cheek." You *felt* all that but you didn't say it. Now, when you *say* it, an additional something happens.

This is the opening page of the original manuscript of "Tropic of Cancer" just as I typed and corrected it. It has traveled a long way from the Paris of 1932 to the special collections room of the UCLA library.>

I am living in the Villa Seurat, the guest of Michael Fraenkel. There is not a crumb of dirt anywhere, nor a chair misplaced. We are all alone here and we are dead.

~~Not~~ Last night Michael discovered that he was lousy. I had to shave his arm-pits and even then the itching did not stop. How can one get lousy in a beautiful place like this? But no matter. ~~We had a wonderful conversation later.~~ We might never have known each other so intimately had it not been for the lice.

Michael has just given me a brief summary of his philosophy. He is ~~a meteorologist,~~ a weather prophet. The weather will continue bad, he says. There will be more calamities, more death, more despair. ~~There is~~ Not the slightest indication of a change anywhere. The cancer of time is eating us away. Our heroes have killed themselves or are killing themselves. The hero, then is not Time, ~~as he was for Proust~~ but Timelessness. Th~~e book of the day is "Werther's Younger Brother." Everything else is false, of no value, a bad accent, a borken rhythm.~~ We must get in step, a lock-step, toward the prison of death. There is no escape. The weather will not change.

There's an actual sensation, which might be related to a physical sensation, involved in words and the use of words. Very definitely. Words are far different from other media. I have great reverence for the word because behind it lies what I call magic. The creation of the word is an absolutely mysterious thing. We don't know anything about the origins of language. Man has never been able to describe how it was that he learned to speak. They try to tell you that first he barked like an animal, and this and that, but I don't believe that. I feel there's something far more mysterious and magical about it. So when you are using words, if you are an unconscious artist and a creative individual, you are aware of this all the time. And words, by the way, can carry you into action, carry you into thought, instead of the other way around.

Now, of course, all this—the sensation and the sensual feeling—lies in the descriptive quality, the use of adjectives and adverbs for color. Here's a strange thing—one writer will describe accurately whatever it is that he's talking about and it doesn't hit you. It bores you, puts you to sleep. Another one uses, what shall I say, metaphors. He doesn't enumerate and specify. Once again, it comes back to the magic of words, the use of words. It isn't the words themselves, it's how they are juxtaposed, and therein lies the skill of the creative artist. It's *what* words are put together and *how* they are put together, what they *evoke*, not what they *say*. This is the whole business of the art of writing.

The satisfaction of the writer, more so than that of the reader is, once again, an individual thing. I'm sure that some writers agonize over their work. Other writers—I can put myself in that category—enjoy it. I enjoy it as it flows out of me. I say, "If only so-and-so could see me now, see this stuff coming off the typewriter, he'd enjoy it." But this varies greatly with individuals. Some men write line

by line, stop, erase, take the sheet out and tear it up, and so on. I don't proceed that way. I just go on and on. Later, when I finish my stint, I put it, so to speak, in the refrigerator. I don't want to look at it for a month or two, the longer the better. Then I experience another pleasure. It's just as great as the pleasure of writing. This is what I call "taking the ax to your work." I mean chopping it to pieces. You see it now from a wholly new vantage point. You have a new perspective on it. And you take a delight in killing even some of the most exciting passages, because they don't fit, they don't sound right to your critical ear. They may have been wonderful to write but as a critic you view them in a different light. I truly enjoy this slaughterhouse aspect of the game. You may not believe it, but it's true.

Here is another corrected page from "Tropic of Cancer." This is one of those pages that the prurient minded never miss. >

in her valise. Immense, avec les choses inouies. Rona now, she had a cunt. I know it because she sent us some hairs from down there. Rona, Rona... a wild ass snuffing pleasure out of the wind. On every high hill she played the harlot, and sometimes in telephone booths and toilets. She bought a bed for King Fredl and a shaving mug. She lay in Tottenham Court Road with her dress pulled up and fingered herself. She used candles, Roman candles, and door knobs. Not a prick in the land big enough for her, not one. Men went inside her and curled up. She wanted extension pricks, self-exploding rockets, hot boiling oil made of wax and creasote. She would cut off your prick and keep it inside her forever, if you let her. One cunt out of a million, Rona! A laboratory cunt and no litmus paper that could take her color. She was a liar, too, this Rona. She never bought the bed for King Fredl. She crowned him with a whisky bottle and her tongue was full of lice and to-morrow. Poor Fredl, he could only curl up inside her and die. She had only to draw a breath and he fell out of her. Enormous fat letters, avec les choses inouies. A valise without straps. A hole without a key. And she spoke German, too. She had a German mouth, French ears, Russian ass. Cunt international. When the flag waved it was red all the way back to the throat. You entered on the Boulevard Jules Ferry and came out at Porte de la Villette. You dropped your sweetbreads into the tumbrils. Red tumbrils with two wheels. At the confluence of the Ourcq and the Marne, where the water sluices through the dykes and lays like glass under the birdges. Rona is lying there now and the canal is full of glass and splinters, the mimosas weep

Hemingway, they say, was a man who corrected his work the following day. And Thomas Mann even corrected his the same day. He wrote one page every day, I am told, and corrected it the same day. He turned out a massive production in this way. Every day without fail he wrote one page. Jesus, in 365 days, you've got a volume! I find that very, very difficult to do. Impossible, rather. But there it is again—who knows what machinery is at work in each individual, how it works? Each man is unique.

Editors are anathema to me. I have never allowed any editor to do any editing of my work. (Most editors are failed writers.) I don't agree with their opinions nor do I want to hear them. I don't want anything except what *I* said, whether good or bad. I don't want any improvements made by somebody else. I understand that today, for instance, there are young writers whose work an editor may like but he insists on making changes. So, the manuscript is given to a re-write man who makes the necessary changes. When the book is published, whose book is it?

I've run into this situation only in America. No editor in Europe has ever dared to do that or suggest it. But here I meet with it constantly. Magazine editors are the worst offenders. They say, "Don't you think this paragraph would be better here instead of there?" And I say, "No, I don't. Take it or leave it." European authors aren't bothered with such stupidities. We have a notion here of perfection, but perfection is equated to sales. They want to please the average reader. They think they know what people want. I don't think they know their ass from their elbow.

Some readers and critics contend that there is a contradiction between myself as writer and as person. But they never knew me as an individual. I believe I describe myself pretty closely in my books. There's the sensual me, the philosophical me, the religious me, the aesthetic me. I like to regard myself as many-faceted, and if one doesn't notice it in my conversation it could be because of circumstance. When I think back to my days in Paris with certain bosom friends and how we talked, it was a totally different kind of conversation. I can talk on many different levels. I can talk gutter language and I can talk like an angel, if you like. It's all one come Christmas, so to speak.

A corrected page from the original manuscript of "Tropic of Cancer." >

that he leaves this esoteric world and adopts the pragmatism of William James & Co.

The other night Van Norden was in his spiritual mood, ~~again.~~ His ~~Danish~~ Georgia cunt had been sleeping with him again. ~~Why did he take her back? Out of pity, it seems.~~ He laughs softly and then he says: "Did you ever sleep with a woman who had her hair shaved off? It's funny, isn't it? Sort of mad-like. She made me so curious that I got up and turned my flashlight on it. And what's there? ~~The more I examined it, the more philosophical I got.~~ Just a crack, ~~I says to myself--two thin pieces of meat--and that's what we burn ourselves up about! They're all alike. That's what makes it funnier.~~ Just a crack that you stick your penis into. And the rest is illusion, lies, imagination. I looked at it a long while. I made her take her two fingers and open it wide ...you know the funny little dewlaps? Jesus, I had to laugh. ~~Nothing...nothing.~~ You expect maybe ~~that~~ you're going to discover something. But there's nothing...nothing. It would be cute if there was a harmonica inside, or a calendar. But all that mystery--and then nothing...nothing. ~~It drives me wild to think about it.~~ I think it's the hair that makes it mysterious." ~~Listen, I got so disgusted that I turned my back on her and read a book. You can get something out of a book, even out of the worst book....."~~

CHARACTERS

Challacombe
Dewar
Schneider
Einstein
Stanley
Wright
O'Regan
Tom Ogden
Father
Jack Lawton
Tillotson
Berg
Hartman
Tomajiro Asai
Frank Reilly
Wardrop
Burger
Grimm
Steve Hill
Charles Fisch
Jim Thornton
Poindexter
L'Estrange
Platé
Lou Jacobs
Lionel Allyn
Stockham
Ed. Perry
Urbanski
Hubert Harrison
Chuckie Morton
Harry Martin
George Wilson
Charlie Sullivan
Baron de Planta
Geo. Kammelkamp
Chas. Baxter
H. W. + Albert Hendricks
Fred Chase
Major Carew
[illegible]

Cora Seward
Louise Ashley
Frances Hunter
Helen Sullivan
Edna Booth
Ida Lane
Aunt Emilie
Anna Wagensch[...]
Florence Marti[n]
Miss Carpenter
Louise Carmen
Lottie Jacobs
Norma Burger
Mrs. A. C. Burg[er]
Gertrude Imho[ff]
Jennie Main
Lillian Fisch

males—(Cont.)
Baron de Planta
Jimmy Pasta
Benjamin Fay Mi[lls]
George Kammelka[mp]
Karl Karsten
Paul Kerls

IDEAS

Obsession for philosophy + religio[n]
Grappling with life-work
Disgust + contempt for parents + rel[atives]
Glamour of Sex
Dislike for alcohol
Hatred for clergy + reformers
Romanticism concerning Cora
Effects of Pauline's age on my lov[e]
Strong friendships—Dewar, Wright, St[anley]
Dewar's strange influence—for evi[l]
Desires for purity and scholarship
Puny gropings as literary artist
Complete absorption in Hobs
Effects of first great music—Bach
Idealization of desert life—Arizona
The body beautiful—physical culture
Morbid sensitiveness—suicide mania
Railings against parenthood
Objections to educational trends
Effects of Bergson's philosophy
Hatred for industrial life—ugliness
Ideas of self-sacrifice for noble cause
Terrific results of loving Cora
Chivalric sacrifice for Pauline

These are some of the people, ideas and incidents I told myself I must include when writing my "autobiographical romances." The unbelievable thing is that most of this material was incorporated in these books.

DESCRIPTIVE BITS

e Old Neighborhood – Costume settings
athers Shop – 5 W. 31 St
e Wolcott Bar
mma Goldman's meetings
ree-for-all forum at Madison Square Garden
om Sharkey's Saloon
aily walk from Delancey St. to shop
he Pre-war Tenderloin district
ix Day Bike Race – Bravo!
meeting of the Xerxes Society
ew Year's Day in Greenpoint
aking Cora Seward – violets
rench Whorehouse at Herald Square
etting drunk with Al Dewar
hilosophizing with Challacombe at Gilford's
on Jacob's home
oliday feast at Helen's or Smith's
uneral and feast at Lutheran Cemetery
isiting Imhofs at Glendale & Bensonhurst
attery A – Heavy Artillery – Irving Sq. Ch
eturn to Pauline from California
ffair in gallery at Parsifal performance
dna Booth in Catskill Mountains
imes Square – open forum – early part of War
[illegible] with Henry Ammann – "Weenie"
hing Aunt Emilie to lunatic asylum
[illegible]

Where am I

What am I doing

Sarlat - Book store (nostradamus)
Dordogne (St. Anthème = nostradamus)
Saint Rémy - Salon (nostradamus)
The Roussillon { Banyuls / Collioure Perpignan / Perpignan
Prades (Casals) - "Le Canigou"
(Vincent - fleas in church)
Hamburg (Transvestists)
(Swedish Consul + wife)
Copenhagen - Bibalo in hospital with piano
Forte dei Marmi (Italian Sculptor) (Marino Marini)
Viarregio - Matisse - Yacht!
London - Perlès (Interview)
Ireland - Alf + wife (Oscar Wilde + John Wayne)
Dublin, Cork, Killarney, Limerick
Galway + Connamara (Arizona)
Formentor - Mallorca
Ping Pong with Carlo Levi
* Jefferson City, Mo. (Penitentiary)
Paris - Reunion with Rattner, (James Jones & wife)
Brassai, Belmont etc.
Ionesco at Le Vesinet.
Percha - Hildegard Neff
Tour Bavaria with actor (michel mininger) + musician brother.
{ Ludwig's Castles
Salzkammergut!
Jack Bilbo at his "Spielunke" (Berlin)
Grosz Exhibition - "
Copenhagen - first etchings!
Rochester, Minn. (Mayo Clinic) (Insane Asylum) (murals in waiting halls)
Edinburgh Festival (the novel!)
Chicago - Chez Elmer Gertz
Rattner's stained glass window in Loop Synagogue
Ireland! (Vive les clochards!)
* Children begging in rain - outside Lisbon
Wells, England - Surrealist facade of cathedral ("The Swans") - at 4th PM Punkt!
Hildegard Knef = Transvestite Saloon (Berlin)
(The client who wanted to protect her!)
Chez Pierre Lesdain - with Eve, Elch, Rouse
Woluwe - St. Lambert (Brussels)
The Beech tree forest leading to "the admirable Ruysbroeck" Monastery - the great mystic
- Bruges - The Dead City (for Poets)
Amsterdam - Hotel with Val, Tony, + Gerald R. Play acting at table!
- The Mystic Lamb of Van Eyck at Ghent (Belgium)
The town where Eleanora Duse was born!
Small French town - où suis-je?
(Steel about India)

Glendale, L.I. (...)
Fallsburgh, N.Y. (Blind Mr. Walker)
Blue Point, L.I. (Swartswood Lake, N.J.)
Bike Races - Jamaica Turnpike
Lake Pocotopaug - Connecticut
* Imperial City, Calif. (Loss of identity) *
San Diego - Emma Goldman = Nietzsche! (Anti-Christ)
Dragor (Poet Laureate)
Sète Paul Valéry's Tomb - I and dog's double! avec Ledig
Chaos (Gard) - John Bohn
Pont du Gard (Paul Morand)
Pont Saint Esprit (Roosevelt)
Toulouse* (Dream - Insanity) (*dead writer and phone book)
Elsinore (with kids)
Die (Drôme) - Tony talking French
Sommières - Durrell (dinner in tent)
Camargue (mosquitos)
Aigues-Mortes - Statue of Louis!
Uzès (Village idiots - French writers)
Cannes (the hotel - double mirror) (the crazy girls)
Montpellier - Temple + Delteil
Eze-sur-Mer (Nietzsche's double!)
La Ciotat - Michel Simon (his domestics) no water
Feltrinelli's crazy chateaux
Lucca (the women) + churches
Pisa (talking to tower all hours)
Simenon - chateau at Echandens (Charlie Chaplin)
Minden (Hannover) - father's ancestors
Bremen (mother's) "
Darmstadt (Keyserling - Valentin meeting)
Reinbek - {Die Schmiede (Prof. of History of art) / Ein Ungebumbelte Füchsdbis}
Rowohlt Verlag
Ping Pong chez
Luneberg Heide (Planet Moon)
Mölln (Til Eulenspiegel) {avec Ledig}
"Just Wild about Harry" (X'mas empty stomach!)
East Berlin - Paris Dress Shop (!)
{Hildegard Knef - Berlin + Munich homes / David Cameron
{Maulbronn - Hermann Hesse / Baden-Baden - Surrealistic
Florida (ditto)
Pensacola
Liechtenstein (one street - ennui after 2 hours!)
Ouchy - Lausanne - Byron's Hotel (the writer from Pakistan)
Vienna - with Emil + Vince (Brooklyn at worst)
Lisbon - (the Fada - tutti frutti houses) (Portuguese - rum stomach down) = the crazy writer offering the world!
Lugano + Locarno (Paradise)
* Venice - near suicide!
* Verona - my town! (Caliger family)
Assisi - Delteil's St. Francis (bazaars as at Lourdes)
Republic of San Marino - Big Sur!
Biarritz - a bore - rain, rain, rain
The Basque Village nearby (unfriendly)
Valladolid - Salamanca (Cervantes)
San Sebastian - very alive!
St. Plantons (Gascony) - the meal!

Never ... (never ...)
Lhasa
Mecca
Timbuctoo
Samarkand
Ispahan

Charleston, S.C. (Nîmes)
Biloxi, Miss. - Live oaks (1 mile
New Iberia, La. - Weeks Hall
Grand Canyon (still the best!)
Synagogues: {Prague / Toledo / Seville / Loop - Chicago
(Moses Maimonides)
Verona and Cordova (my favorite towns)
Wells (England) - the Surrealist facade of Cathe... (The Swans - Punkt...
The Vatican - Ugliest ... (Fit of laughter) avec ...
Montagnola (Hermann He...
What city was it which was stronger in dream = remembrance than actuality ???
Les Baux (Les frères)
Chickamauga - Stanley Boro... Col. Felix G.
Café Boudon - Paris (Rue Fontaine = Algerian ... Hon Gilotte
El Greco's dining Room (Toledo) - and S...
Corfu - the General's mistre...
Corfu - violating temple (...
Nice - The Negro bootblac...
Bowling Green, Va.
Caresse drunken deserter
Salvador Dali + Gala
Isère (Van Gogh billiard pa... introuvable 2ème fois!
Chimney Rock, N.C. and Somewhere in Tennessee (2 best meals in U.S. - 75¢)
The feast at La Pyramide (M. et Mme Point)
Tubingen - nobody knows ...

When I write by hand I'm more sincere. That's because I'm getting away from my "literary" self. The moment I sit at a typewriter my fingers are already activating me, altering me, putting me in the groove of the writer. When I take up the pen it's a little more cumbersome, more awkward, unnatural, so there isn't that same facility. I'll give you an example. Picasso often said about his work that when he is through with a painting, if there were some things in it that were lovely and charming, he would cut them out because those were expressions of his facility. What he wants is something that comes out of his guts, that he struggles with, something that isn't just pleasing. I am naturally more literary when I write with a typewriter. Things come out more glibly, more polished too. Whereas with the pen it's a struggle, and the material seems to come from a different source.

With talk it varies a great deal. It's like a flood, a cataract, with some people. With others, I hem and haw or I grow silent. It's how people touch you off, and in what areas. It depends on whom I'm up against, how relaxed I am, and whether I feel in good form and am in a good mood, whether I can reveal and express myself. It's dependent upon all sorts of things. I know that I'm somewhat of an actor and I know that all of us are dishonest to a degree—in the sense that we are actors. We know how good we are, or think we are, or we want to make an impression, and all these things color our speech. If you're talking to a girl whom you want to impress, whom you're madly in love with, and you talk to another girl who doesn't mean a goddamn thing to you, everything changes, doesn't it? So it is with men. Some men you want to get close to, or you want to open them up, or you want to impress them. You feel inferior or superior, all sorts of things. There's such a multitude of factors involved when we confront one another.

Here are the names of places in various parts of the world where mysterious things happened to me. I am one of those people to whom things happen. In National City, California, near the Mexican border, for example, I experienced for the first time a complete loss of identity.

In talking face to face with someone I have had the desire to express a thought earnestly and sincerely and suddenly I have found myself lying, or distorting the thought to suit a momentary whim. I think I understand and recognize a lot about myself. And what is there to be ashamed of? There is no absolutely honest man. Everything is mixed, "grayish," not just black and white.

If I wrote on a typewriter about a certain experience, and then I wrote a letter to someone about the same experience, or talked in person to him about this experience, each version would be different. What you leave out or what you put in is a matter of selection. Now with the machine I feel that I give myself to the fullest. In talking I may give another full expression but with a deeper note of sincerity.

Whether consciously or not, when I write a letter in longhand I am probably coming close to talk. Because I do want to reveal myself. But when you talk about revealing, you naturally think about talk, talking it out with someone, telling someone about something.

orders for Cossery's "Men God Forgot"

1. 7 Stairs Book Shop (Chicago) – Frick — 10 copies – 40%
2. Red Door Book Shop " – " (Paid) — 10 " "

Outline of "Tropic of Capricorn"

Note: "On the Ovarian Trolley"

Background – antecedents – philosophy of life – desire to live imaginatively (rather than seek "Truth") – against work (Jack Lawson's death) – Desperate always – Looking for work – a pastime. Western Union job (p. 19–50). Valeska ~~...~~ Govern (Sunset Place)

Note: – (See how "waybills" is translated in French version – p. 27 top!) Mallory (Catholic Welfare League. Real names of goofy mgrs. mentioned (cases). Always broke – Swindling blind newspaper man for carfare

Note: – p. 32: "Once we did get a bonus and Hymie took me to Delmonico's" (sic!) "Dave Olinski" (pp. 40–41)

Note: – The Horatio Alger first book! Ulric – friends – loads of them, all despise the other friends! (Talk of Paris – descriptions) "Just a Brooklyn Boy!"

Note: – cor. 6th ave + 49th St: Europe! Kronski and my "euphorias"! Hymie – "ovaries". Book of the hours – Same book always (in the head!) Fantasy on Hymie the bull-frog! (p. 55–57). Love for the old things. "Should have been a clown!" My irritating talk! (Persona non grata)

Note: – Valeska + her nigger blood. Borrowing money of her. Playing domino tricks with child while B. gets abortion. Valeska table [illegible]. Sense of desolation – wrong birthday + hour! "always dragging behind", etc. (Born with crucifixion complex") A fanatic!

Note – Beyond crucifixion – becoming "gay" (p. 67–8) "Live like a rock!" O'Rourke + nocturnal rambles thru streets. "Whoever thru too great love...." (p. 72.) One man in me that had died! Walking around

* in center of chaos! More on telegraph rigmarole (Chaos) – pp. 74–8

~~End of Part I~~

Note – Valeska + Lesbian midget (hermaphrodite) – Girl upstairs (no name) – Sexual affair (p. 79) – "I wanted to be alone for a thousand years – in order to forget!" Note this ending!!!

End of Part I. (p. 78)

Note: Pauline Janowski + Balzac. Telegram from "Monica" (~~waitress~~). Love letters. Her erudition. Egyptian corpse at Grand Central. "It's me, Izzy". Death of Kronski's first Jewess episode (Kronski) wife – Yetta. Walk thru Prospect Park with him – His crazy talk! Des. of our German funerals, by contrast.

Capricorn notes —out.

p. 351 — Truth — is only the core of a totality which is inexhaustible"

* p. 352 — Letter to Mara telling of book about her I am going to write!

*Note (Perhaps in Introd. to R.C. mention this — and notes done at Park Comm's office.)

the whole page!

p. 353 — The first girl I loved! (Una Gifford) Note well this passage!

p. 354 — The widow! — long exposition of relationship.

p. 357 — The day I "walked out on the old life" (at W. U.) — "I was 30 then! (see age given in R.C.!!)

p. 358 — Description of Mara "coming towards me" at dance hall.

p. 359 — "Henriette" (Strindberg) — is this in "Miss Julie"

(Finished Sept. 1938)

Perhaps quote also (front of R.C.) this from p. 261 of Capricorn: "All this that is going on, all music, all architecture, all law, all government, all invention, all discovery — all this is velocity exercises in the dark, Czerny with a capital Zed riding a crazy white horse in a bottle of mucilage."

*

---

compare Biblical quotes (Grover Watrous = Capr.) with Crazy George in R.C.

---

p. 94 (R.C.) Kronski's talk — cp with "Psycho. section" — repeated!

p. 251 — (R.C) — Almost repetition of scene with "candle + wheelbarrow" Ulric + schoolmistress —

p. 277 (R.C.) Meetings with personnel mgrs — See if not related in Capricorn?

---

* NOTE Tell Girodias not forget American + English copyrights on "R.C."! "No par. sent. or phrases to be quoted without permission!"

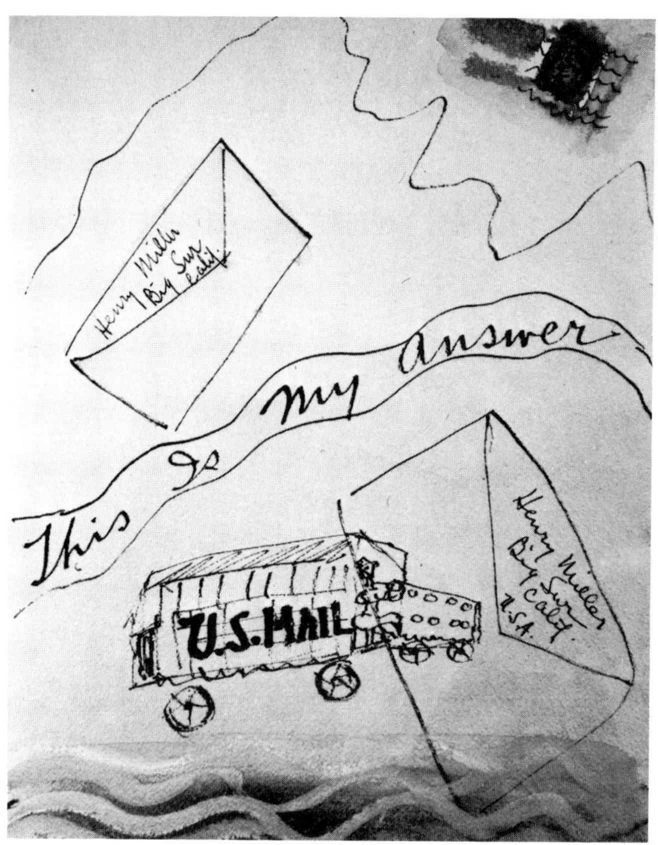

I haven't the faintest idea why I did this, but I have the habit of decorating letters and envelopes when I am in good fettle.

With writing there has got to be something more, some added quality. In writing there is also acting. You are usually conscious of where you're going. They talk about writers going into trances. Sure, I've been through that. Words came out of me from nowhere, everywhere. I was the "victim" of these words. It was like a hose opening up with words pouring down on me and I just transmitted them to paper. Those are glorious moments and terrible ones too, because you can't turn the damn thing off. I used to beg, "Stop it! Stop it! Leave me alone!" But that doesn't happen every day. God help us if it did, because we'd be dead from exhaustion.

About this element of the actor in writing.... He's putting a face on things, and he is also facing the world. He doesn't see the world out there definitely but he knows it's listening. Just like a virtuoso on stage. I really think there's something to this. On the other hand, when writing a letter to a friend you try to be sincere. When you talk to someone it's a little of both. It's an act again. When I face someone it can bring out certain thoughts I would never have if I were facing the machine or if writing a letter.

I don't think a writer feels good because he's reliving an experience. I think he feels good because he's able to transcribe the experience onto paper. It's the ability to recapture that makes you happy, not the actual reliving. I think the reliving is secondary. It is for me anyway. My joy is in the accomplishment. At least that's the way it seems to me. If you think it may be the way I *want* it to seem, that's an unconscious thing on my part. And that does creep in, no question about it.

I struggled in the beginning. I said I was going to write the truth, so help me God. And I thought I was. I found I couldn't. Nobody can write the absolute truth. It's impossible. Your ego won't permit it. I think the truth is something that slides through your fingers. You can't capture it. Maybe you capture it in the silence with your own self, at moments, and even then very seldom. I think we live lies. All of us. We never live face to face with the reality about ourselves.

When I look back at myself, I don't see *a* self. I see many selves. Sometimes I am surprised by a certain self that I reveal. We are not a single self all the time; we don't go through that wonderful evolution, upward and onward. It's a zigzag thing, up and down—there's no wonderful soul moving ahead that you can describe.

Ideas — 1938

Jan. Get "Un Etre Etoilique" translated into Chinese and then back again into English. Three versions in one book.

Book of "Some Pleasant Monsters" — Fred, Edgar, Osborn, Fraenkel.
Book in bad French — "Tout S'arrangera".
Book of Essays etc — "Plasma and Miasma".
Osborn's Collected Poems — with preface + photos.

Feb. ~~7th~~ 10th Do 5 pages a day of Capricorn regularly

Day passed going to movies with the Durrells!

Begin to-morrow!!

2/18/38 — not yet begun!

2/17/38 = Get "Aller Retour" published in 6 languages in the one volume (French, German, Dutch, Spanish, Italian, Russian, Chinese)

2/18/38. Note: astrological forecast for "Capricorn" arrived to-day from Joe O'Regan, just when I had written "I must have music at all costs" — "The C minor Quartet of Beethoven! and the book, "I Ching".
(coincidence)

3/8/38 Important meeting with Moricand this evening — 9[30] – 11[00] P.M.

Publish "Land of Fuck" privately in

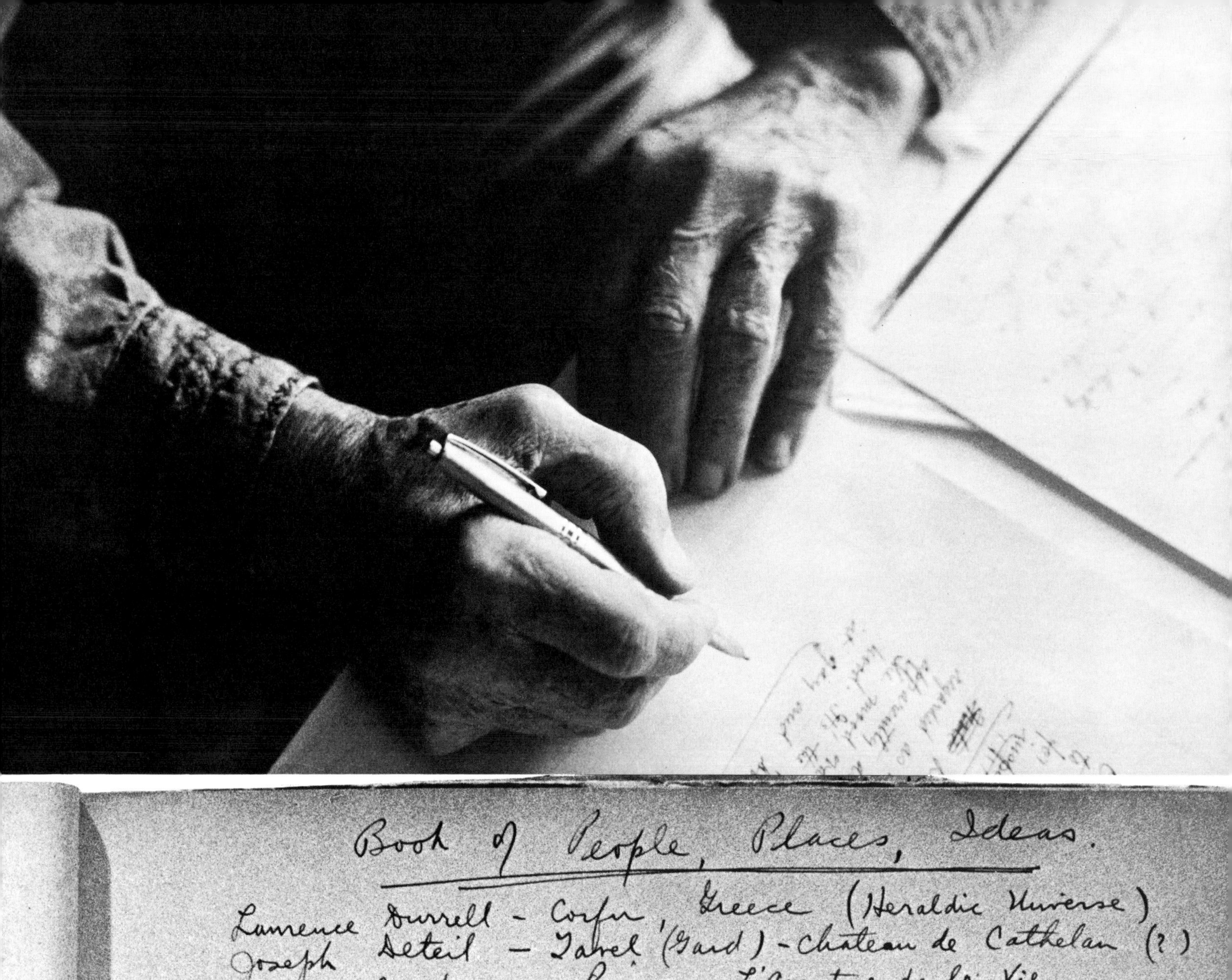

Book of People, Places, Ideas.

Lawrence Durrell - Corfu, Greece (Heraldic Universe)
Joseph Delteil - Tarel (Gard) - Chateau de Cathelan (?)
Blaise Cendrars - Paris - L'Aventure de la Vie
Conrad Moricand - " - Astrology
Charles albert Cingria - " - Music
Raymond Thiberge - " - Automatisim
Count Hermann Keyserling - Darmstadt (Meaning & Express
Michael Fraenkel - Mexico City - Hamlet
David Edgar - Paris - Neurosis
Dr. C. J. Jung - Zurich - The Super Ego
Henri Matisse - Nice - World of Color
Artur Lundkvist - Copenhagen - Surréalisme chez les nordi
Knut Hamsun - Norway - Romance
T. S. Eliot - London - Neo-Catholicism
Evreinov - Paris - The Theatre
Antonin Artaud - " - The Drama
Belgian Painter - The Grand Old Man! (Neptune
Hans Reichel - Paris - The Birds & the Fishes
Jean Giono - Manosque - Midi

Bring in smoked sturgeon!! Maybe some one will send some!

Miscellany

Never read (asked) Nick Carter, Jesse James, Buffalo Bill. Sherlock Holmes (Weekly Serials) — bored me!

Art of Conversation – nil in America. Always head on vs. indirect. Say "Yes" first, then ——. As young man, if I made a statement, it was always – "You must be crazy!" Sure I was crazy – stark crazy! – to argue with fools + nincompoops.

Callers: "Loved that where you say.... but when you go into...." etc. They came to tell me – not to see if perhaps they were mistaken or had misunderstood.

"People are – or So+So is – all right, up to a point". Nuts! Either OK all thru or no! Guy who is OK. up to a point is usually no fucking good. Take the whole man, the whole work(s) — and find the green parsley!

List books, + brochures – and articles (foreign reviews) written since Big Sur

---

The nobodies who do the dirty work – "archons"?

Monthly postage bill almost equals monthly royalties from N.D. (at least last year!) $450

✓ Visitors who notice nothing! who don't make up to children or dogs. Leery of them!

✓ Drunk from "Time" (with Virginia + Elena Rex) staggered by Val – beautiful – coming out of room to make pipi

---

Best day at Big Sur – abalone, pool in forest, dinner, dancing, with Paco. Hugh + Margaret and Tony reading – Manila Meyrose

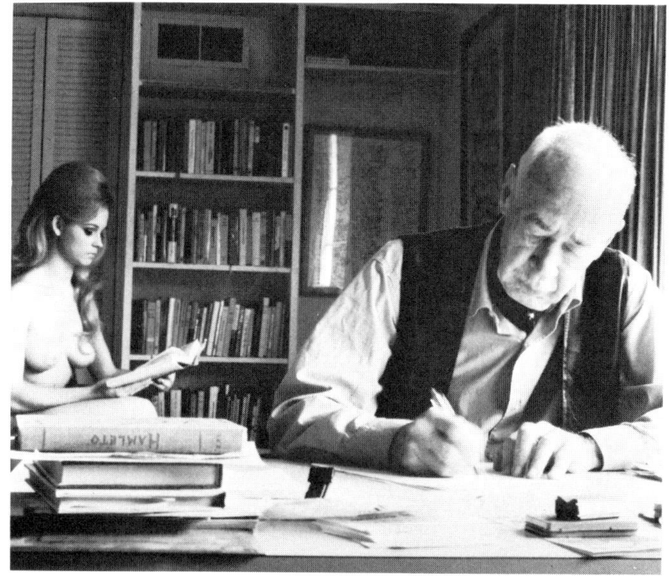

When I write about something funny I don't stop and think about writing something humorous. I don't have prepared thoughts. I'm just putting it down, and if it turns out humorously or sadly it's beyond my control. I'm not thinking about effects, not usually. And talking about effect, sometimes when I'm doing a descriptive bit I may stop and think about the effect. I might say, "Put this in, put that down, take that out." Because it's more effective. But not when I'm writing about my feelings. They come out as they are. If it's funny, it's funny, if it's not, it's not. Many times, while writing, I laugh. I laugh out loud.

When I was young, I would be exultant one day and depressed the next. In later life from the middle forties on, I was on a more serene level. I always like to use the word "acceptance." It's a very big word for me. Accepting life as it is, seeing what it is, and taking it for what it is, not having illusions and delusions about it. When I got rid of my "idealism" that was a big step, I would say, toward health. In Rabelais' "Gargantua" there is inscribed over the portal of the Abbaye de Thélème, "Fay ce que vouldras!" "Do as you please!" in other words. St. Augustine put it another way. He said, "Love God and do as you please." How wonderful! It means that spirit, the Holy Spirit, is important—not morals, not ethics. If one is imbued with the right spirit one can't do wrong. Then to do as one pleases can only bring happiness—to oneself and to one's fellow man.

I think I wrote about sex because it was such a big part of my life. Sex was always the dominant thing. To be honest, I haven't written much about my real loves. Some of them, the real loves in my life, I haven't mentioned in my books at all. And I've only tried to cover a certain period of time in the books—seven or eight years with one woman, June, or Mona in the books. And then impulsively I branched out in all directions. But that was my main objective, to tell about my life with her.

The funny thing about pornographic writing is that it doesn't stimulate me. It doesn't have much effect on me at all. In fact, I'd say it's boring to me. It's true that I haven't read very many of the famous classics in this realm, nor do I know why I wasn't drawn to them. I'm a bit of a *voyeur*. Pictures, photos, interest me very much. They stimulate me. But reading about sex, no, not so much. Unless it is done by a great artist.

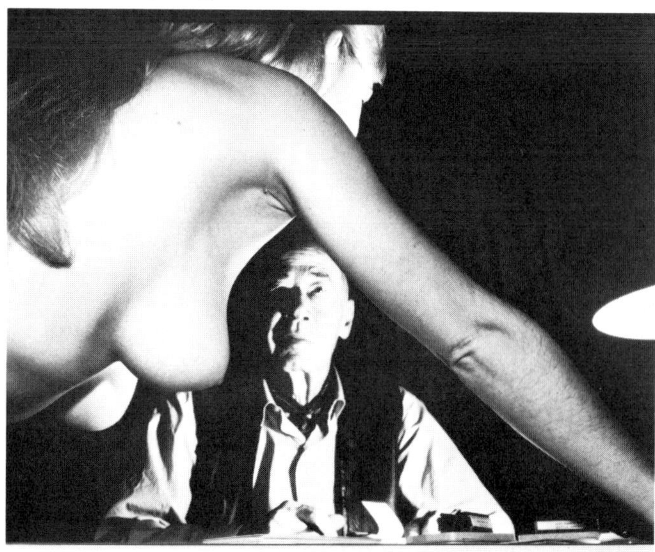

I never celebrate Christmas. It's a holiday that has no meaning for me. Because I like to decorate large sheets of paper with my nonsensical words and pictures I use Christmas as an excuse for giving these away.

X'mas 1969 Shalom!

Dear Joe— The time of the assassins is on us once again. (Praise the Lord!) Peace is everywhere, like some stinking cunt. C-U-N-T. When Obadiah begat Nebuchadnezzar the trouble started. (Don't ask me how!)

Don't forget that J.C. was a Hebe!!! He may even have been circumcised.

And Mary was a Virgin. She was born without a Cunt.

Merry X'mas, ~~Bryo~~ Bryon-San — Byron — How goes it?

(Teeth missing)

From "one of the worst writers that ever lived" (End quote)

Here in the swamps of Pacific Palisades the frogs are croaking all night long. (They sing X'mas carols too, believe it or not.) I have just been playing the first movement of the Leschetitsky Concerto for aches, pains and groans. It's in B-flat minor, with a Coda and a Cadenza. Often played for weddings, circumcisions and blood baths. Every X'mas is a headache. But this one is a block-buster. Only a Paganini or a Thomashersky could survive it. Alles geht schlimmer und schlimmer. Allein ist nicht gut. Man muss Zucchini haben. Und etwas anderes. Fleisch. Hier gibt nur Kohlrabi und Blutwurst.

(Still intact)

Les Crottes

(Clean, polished turds)

(Formerly and Formally Cunt-struck)

The Astonished Heart finds that all is immaculate, holy, inexhaustible, invariable and self-perpetuating. God is not dead—not yet. The angels are eunuchs in disguise. They have no balls but they wear jock straps just the same. Misery is abundant, even in Paradise. Love is at a premium, even when not at par.

When the soul gets rusty use Epsom Salts with a little parsley.

Beware of fools' gold, catnip and claustrophobia. Use the toothpick only when hungry. Keep clear of fat, lard, grease, muck, slime and other residuals. Trust in Jehovah and love all God's creatures, even dogs and cats.

Signed: Henry Foolhardy Miller

In the year of his dotage.

Amen!

We were talking the other day to some Japanese girls. They said they were disgusted with what are called "blue" films. Sheer dirt. I don't agree. I say it's unnatural for anyone to turn his eyes away, no matter how lousy these films are. It's a cock and a cunt and they're fucking and it's exciting! You can't look away. Not if you own a cock or a cunt yourself.

I read the great ones like Casanova, Rabelais, Boccacio, Petronius Arbiter, author of *The Satyricon*, all of which I enjoyed very much as a young man, but I don't think it would be the same today. But *then*, yes, they stirred my blood.

Recently I read a book called *My Secret Life*. This work had been recommended to me a good 20 years ago by our then unacknowledged censor. He said, "Of all the books I've read in that *genre* this to me is the greatest of all." The man who wrote it really loved cunt, you might say. He loved women, purely for sex. He had every kind of woman, it seems. That was all he could think about, really. He had money at his disposal, his time was his own, and I tell you, to read him is exciting because it's just sex and nothing else. There's no literary quality involved. None at all. Just a sheer blow by blow account. I found it exciting at first, but after two or three hundred pages I was bored.

I have never written that way, despite what critics say. That's just it. I went beyond, I exaggerated often, or distorted, because I'm a different type of man. His method of writing would not be enough for me. I have to build, elaborate, fabricate. To me that's the basis of all creation. After all, this sex thing is much more than sex. It's such an elemental force. It's just as mysterious and magical as talking about God or the nature of the universe.

People have said of me that I threw in juicy passages just to keep the reader awake. That isn't true. Judges have said, "He's a good

On this page I have expressed my feelings about the use of language. What I am saying in effect is that there are no dirty words unless people make them so.

If they commence to like him, to take him up, then I will throw Spengler overboard too. We cannot like the same people. We must make new gods, even if every night we are obliged to destroy them. If it is necessary, since language is the medium, we must talk unintelligbly, write unintelligbly. If they are going to take our masculine word "cunt" and fling it about indiscriminately, unfeelingly, then we must invent another term. We must have our own terminology, our own private, essential symbology. They have weakened the whole structure of our society, and now they are trying to poison our words.

I sepak about this with some feeling because of certain things that have happened. I have been accused of being a bad little boy who found delight in using dirty words. I sit around on the terrasse and I hear these dirty words being used wrongly, indelicately. I say these people have no right to use my dirty words, ~~they soil them.~~ they rob them of their strength, their integrity. Back of my dirty words is the strong affirmation of my masculinity, my vitality, my awareness, my reproach against this emasculating world. I put a value on my dirty words: I am not chalking them up on a broker's board to rise one day and fall the next. If my words fail, then I fail. My words are me. My words are sacred. ~~therefore~~ Sacred dirty words, precisely. Not to get holy and sacred before them, but to take them sacredly. I stand behind every dirty word I have used, like an advertiser behind his hole-proof socks. I will exchange them if they are

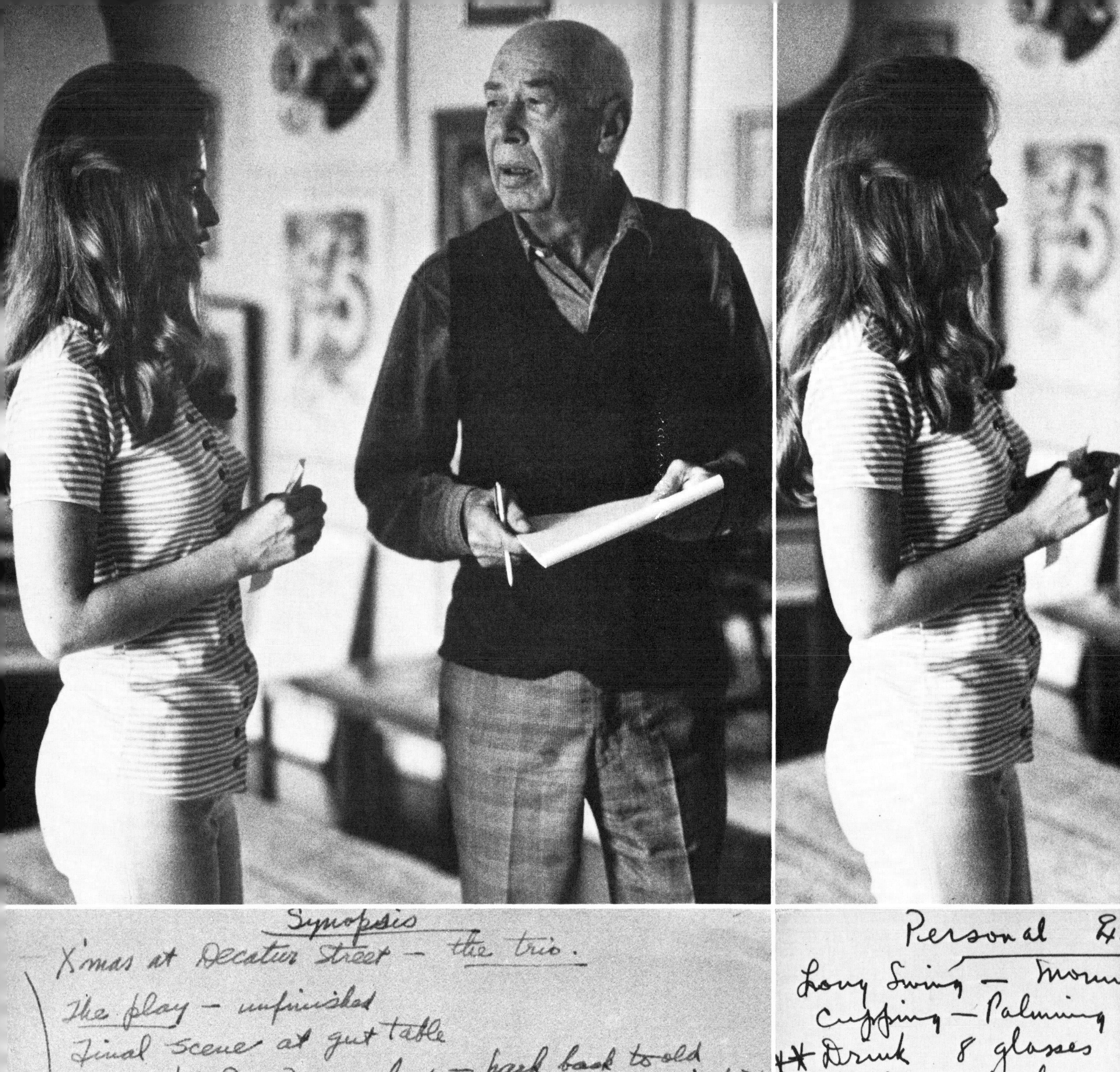

Synopsis

X'mas at Decatur Street — the trio.

The play — unfinished
Final scene at gut table
Visit to Doc Maruchess — hark back to old place in Bklyn — MS. "The Wrestlers". go into it
Jim Londos (little Hercules) Strangler Lewis, Man of a Thousand Holds (Earl Caddock), Jim Driscoll etc.

Looking for job at Ralston's! The crazy veteran.
Bunn Bros. Cafeteria
Talk of Paris! (Mona + Stasia)
Making Death Masks
Stanley's arrival and talk (same line!)
Trying to sell blood
German ticket chopper — pervert.
Sleaco's Birthday — Cabaret!

Visit from Mona's brother. The truth!
Meeting with Jimmy Pasta! — Promise of job.
The night before they leave for Paris.

Personal Ex

Long Swing — Morn
Cupping — Palming
** Drink 8 glasses
Hour's walk before
Read + paint withou
Drink fine wines ev
Type one hour per

Send Tonkunstler (Heath) (3) ex
from "Rosy Cruci

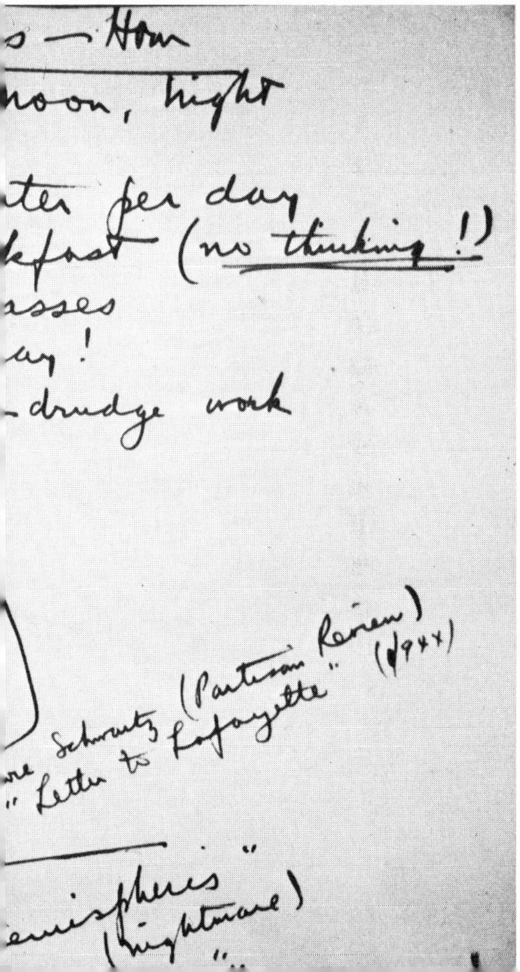

s — How
noon, tight
ter per day
kfast (no thinking!)
sses
ay!
— drudge work

Schwartz (Partisan Review)
"Letter to Lafayette" (1944?)

emispheres"
(nightmare)

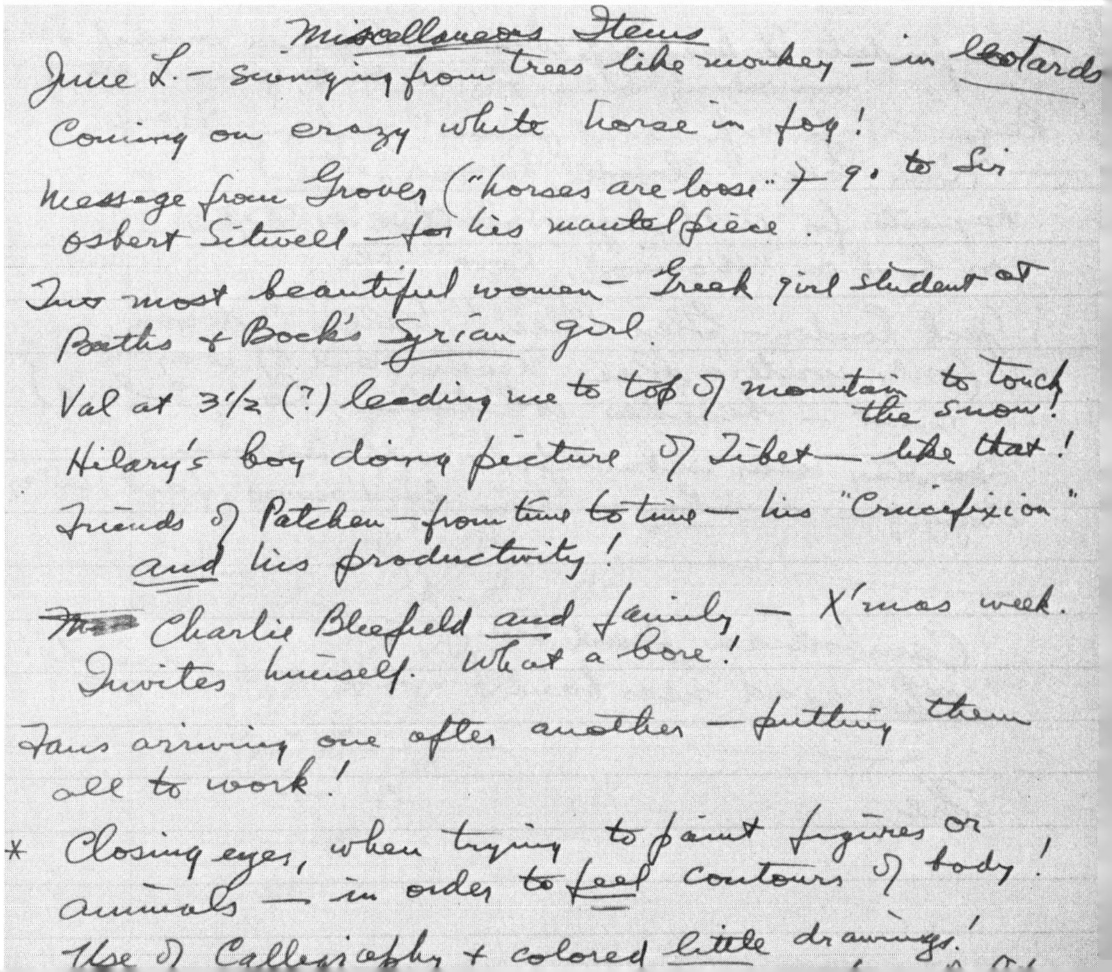

Miscellaneous Items

June L. — swinging from trees like monkey — in leotards
Coming on crazy white horse in fog!
Message from Grover ("horses are loose") to Sir Osbert Sitwell — for his mantelpiece.
Two most beautiful women — Greek girl student at Bathis & Bock's Syrian girl.
Val at 3½ (?) leading me to top of mountain to touch the snow!
Hilary's boy doing picture of Tibet — like that!
Friends of Patchen — from time to time — his "Crucifixion" and his productivity!
Charlie Bleefield and family — X'mas week. Invites himself. What a bore!
Fans arriving one after another — putting them all to work!
* Closing eyes, when trying to paint figures or animals — in order to feel contours of body!
Use of Calligraphy + colored little drawings!

writer but why did he write such things? He did it to make money." I am speaking of those early books where I recount my early life. But my everyday life was full of this objectionable or questionable material. There was so much of it and yet, I suppose, my life wasn't like that of most men. For me sex wasn't an everyday thing. Attached to the woman's cunt was always the woman herself. The *woman* was the most interesting thing. The cunt was important, sure, but that wasn't the whole of it, except in some rare cases. When men refer to a woman as "nothing but a cunt," or rather "all cunt," that's meaningful too. But I was always more interested in the woman, the whole woman. More than that, I'm always interested in the mind. What is she thinking? What is this mind that I'm grappling with? Get at it! Penetrate it! Because in me there's part of the detective. I think I might have made an excellent sleuth had I not become a writer.

But to get back to these objectionable portions of my books, I might even say it was an unconscious bit of artistry on my part to do as I did. Not only that, but I can give you another explanation for these passages. With me one thing leads to another, and very often to something extremely different. I don't have a mind that thinks in a straight line. I explode as I think. I think in many different directions. When I get an idea I go off in many directions at once, and I don't know which one to follow. That's why, often, there is this chaos in my work. I'm exploding, that's what it is.

Another thing. One thing you have to learn in writing is when to call an end, when to write "Finis." I could go on forever. Sometimes I just bring things to an end abruptly.

My notebooks began in the very early days in Paris. I think, in those days, I always carried one with me. I was like a reporter at large. I made notes so conscientiously you'd think I was being paid by a big, important newspaper. I made notes of everything. I kept menus from restaurants, theatre programs, everything. And I pasted a lot of them in the notebooks, all sorts of things. Now, very often, I make no use of my notes, but I enjoy making them. They fire me. Often I'll sit and look at them and then utterly disregard them. But it's something to get me started. It's the same thing with words. I'd fall in love with certain words and then list them on a big sheet of wrapping paper.

Another plan for another unfinished book to be entitled The Palace of Entrails. *This was during the Clichy period when I was working on three or four books at the same time. Greatly influenced by Otto Rank's famous book* Art and Artist.

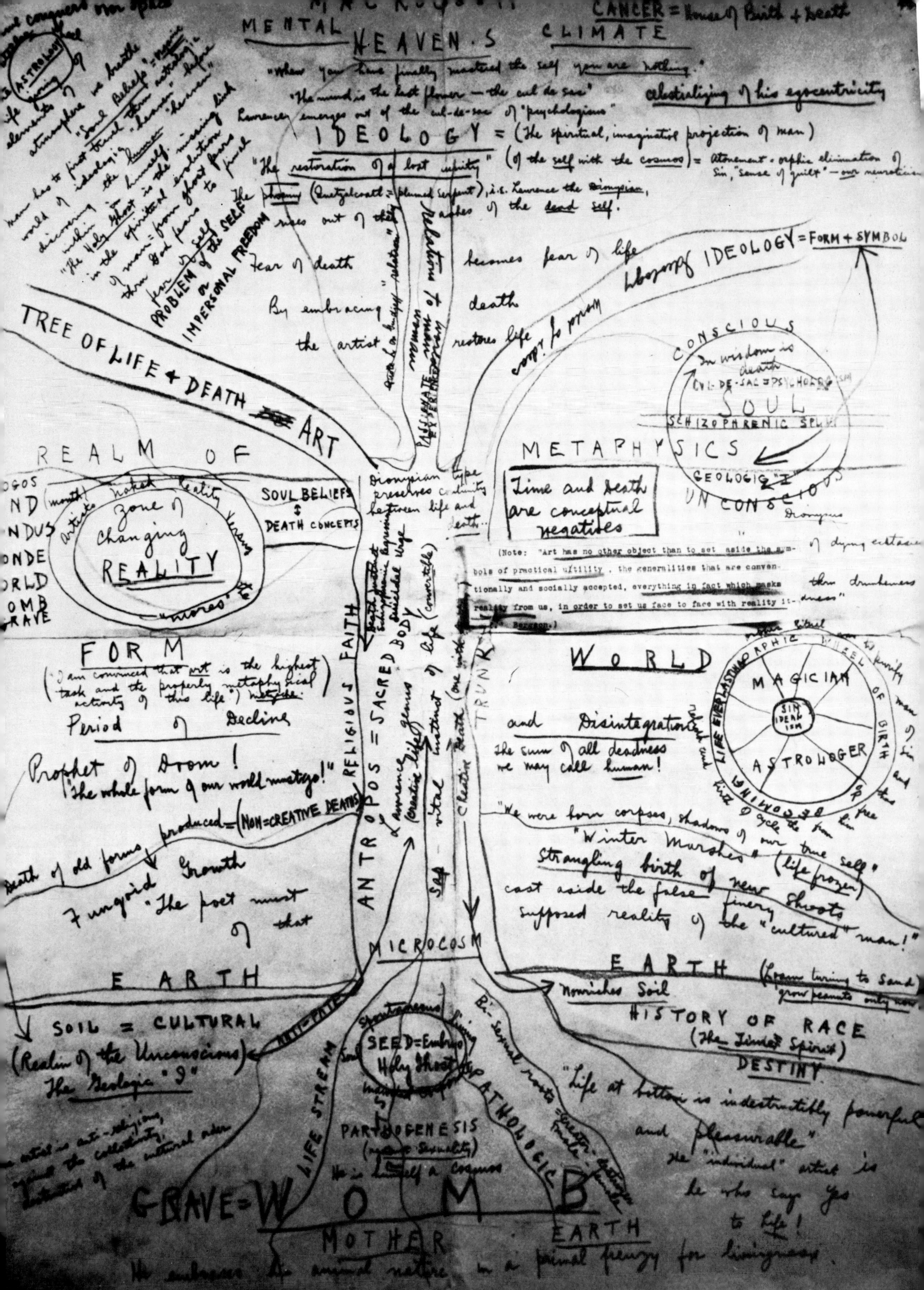

CANCER = House of Birth + Death
MENTAL HEAVEN'S CLIMATE
"When you have finally mastered the self you are nothing."
"The mind is the last flower — the cul de sac"
Celestializing of his egocentricity
Lawrence emerges out of the cul-de-sac of "psychologisms"
IDEOLOGY = (The spiritual, imaginative projection of man)
"The restoration of a lost unity" (of the self with the cosmos) = Atonement = orphic elimination of Sin, "sense of guilt" — our neuroticism
rises out of the ashes of the dead self.
Fear of death becomes fear of life
By embracing death the artist restores life
IDEOLOGY = FORM + SYMBOL
PROBLEM OF THE SELF OR IMPERSONAL FREEDOM
TREE OF LIFE & DEATH
ART
REALM OF
CONSCIOUS
SOUL
SCHIZOPHRENIC SPLIT
GEOLOGIC "I"
UNCONSCIOUS
METAPHYSICS
Time and death are conceptual negatives
Dionysian type preserves continuity between life and death...
SOUL BELIEFS
DEATH CONCEPTS
Zone of Changing REALITY
(Note: "Art has no other object than to set aside the symbols of practical utility, the generalities that are conventionally and socially accepted, everything in fact which masks reality from us, in order to set us face to face with reality itself." Bergson.)
FORM
("I am convinced that art is the highest task and the properly metaphysical activity of this life") Nietzsche
Period of Decline
Prophet of Doom!
"The whole form of our world must go!"
produced = (NON=CREATIVE DEATHS)
Death of old forms
Fungoid Growth
"The poet must
of that
RELIGIOUS FAITH
ANTROPOS = SACRED BODY
TRUNK
WORLD
and Disintegration
The sum of all deadness we may call human!
"We were born corpses, shadows of our true self."
"Winter Marshes" (life frozen)
Strangling birth of new shoots
cast aside the false finery
supposed reality of the "cultured" man!
MAGICIAN
ASTROLOGER
MICROCOSM
EARTH
EARTH
Nourishes Soil
HISTORY OF RACE
DESTINY
SOIL = CULTURAL
(Realm of the Unconscious)
The Geologic "I"
SEED = Embryo Holy Ghost
PARTHOGENESIS
LIFE STREAM
PATHOLOGIC
"Life at bottom is indestructibly powerful and pleasurable"
The "individual" artist is he who says Yes to Life!
He is himself a cosmos
GRAVE = WOMB
MOTHER EARTH
He embraces his animal nature in a primal frenzy for livingness

It was only when I knew I was leaving Paris to go to Greece, and that I might not ever return, that I decided to get those notes bound. And I have many more than what are in the library. Some of my notebooks I gave to people as gifts. I wrote seven books by hand, seven whole books, in printer's dummies, and gave them to friends as gifts. The only one that was ever printed was a little one on Hans Reichel, called *Order and Chaos chez Hans Reichel.* It would be wonderful to see the others printed sometime, although I didn't write them with the intention of having them published.

These books that I wrote for my friends were all written by hand. I usually don't write by hand, except letters. When I write by hand I have the impression that I am more sincere, less literary. The typewriter is too facile for me. It's like practicing scales on the piano. My fingers are somehow working my mind.

I'm hoping to have an easier life. What I want to do is live quietly, peacefully, and work. I want to be forgotten so that I have more peace. I don't need publicity. It causes me misery.

Men don't realize how much a woman can disregard that so-called physical attraction, how they fall for homely, ugly, older men sometimes. Jesus! Sometimes I think these homely bastards get the most beautiful women.

BIG SUR

Sunny days at Big Sur brought out a variety of friends. This was at the shack at Anderson's

All my life it seems I have never chosen the place to live. I've just been put there, by force of circumstance. I didn't choose Big Sur, California, either, though it was the only place in America I could call home.

I left France in June, 1939, to go to Greece. The war broke out while I was in Greece. I was ordered by the American Consul to return to New York. That's where I wrote *The Colossus of Maroussi*. I put my whole heart into that book. I had been in Greece roughly eight or nine months and had found it a Paradise. I had always thought that France was the only country—*my* country. I had even tried to become a citizen of France. At that time one had to pay money to become a citizen and I never had the necessary amount. If I had, I certainly would have become one.

Anyway, when I got to Greece I saw a totally new world. Primarily, it was the world of nature and of sacred places. Never before had I visited places which gave me the feeling that they were sacred. It's so overwhelmingly impressive. You know at first sight that events of untold importance happened here. And then there was the light, the unbelievable light of the Greek sky. It's something I have never seen matched anywhere else.

I went to Greece at the invitation of Lawrence Durrell. He had come to Paris shortly after reading the *Tropic of Cancer*. He had written me a fan letter and a correspondence sprang up. Then one day, a year or so later, he shows up with his young wife. He had been living in Greece for some time already. He kept urging me to go to Greece, where he had a home on the island of Corfu. But I didn't go for several years, and

Creek. Rent was only seven dollars a month, but it was almost forty miles to the grocer.

then only as the war was approaching. I didn't realize even then that the war would come. I thought I would have a year's vacation and return to France. Had the war not intervened I would have stayed in Greece and made it my home. It suited me to a "T."

Well, the war broke out and the American Consul in Athens—who was a rather well-known writer by the way—took my passport, X'd it out and told me I must return to the place I had come from. Naturally I didn't want to return to America, especially New York. I asked him if I could go to South America, or China, anywhere but America... "No!" I had to return to New York. It almost broke my heart. I didn't want to do it, I was through with America. But how strange destiny is! Two years later, I found myself living in Big Sur, another sublime place that, in a way, compared favorably with Greece, *my* Greece. Seventeen years I lived there in Big Sur. And again, what was it? Mountains, sky, sea—only a handful of people. The loneliness of it was marvelous for me.

I was single for a while.

I had just settled in Big Sur, when I received word that my mother was dying, so I went to New York, but my mother didn't die, not then.

While in New York I met a young girl, a graduate of Bryn Mawr who was going to Yale, studying history, or the philosophy of history, rather. Her name was Janina Martha Lepska. She became the mother of our children, Tony and Val. But when I met her she was a girl of 20. I brought her back to Big Sur after being married at the city hall in Denver on the way.

In Big Sur I received royalties now and then but they were very, very meager. I lived very poorly, very cheaply. We had our own vegetable garden and we'd get abalone and fish from the sea. Friends would bring us things. We used to share things with our neighbors. I didn't need much then. I don't remember how much or how little we lived on, but I remember that my friend, Emil White, who came to live there a month after me, lived on about $10 a week. That included everything, rent, food, cigarettes and wine. Figure that out—$10 a week! Times have changed!

I first lived at the place now known as Nepenthe, which was only a log cabin then. I was dropped off one day by a friend of mine who said, "Go there. You've got to see Big Sur and Lynda (Sargent) will probably invite you to stay awhile." And she did. She was a warm and wonderful woman, this Lynda Sargent. I wrote and painted and she cooked the meals—on a wood stove! I stayed as her guest for two months or more. Then she got worried that I might be on her hands for good! I had no money. I was literally a beggar. She helped me find a place to stay, a cabin belonging to the then mayor of Carmel, Keith Evans. He offered me the cabin for $10 a month. If I couldn't pay that he told her I could have it for nothing. I stayed at his place on Partington Ridge for a year.

Lepska, my third wife and mother of my children, Val and Tony. Here she is dancing with Emil. In the early days our pleasures were few and simple.

It was during this time that I went back to New York to see my mother and came back with a new wife. About a year later my daughter, Valentine was born. Then the mayor came back from the war and I had to get out of his cabin. We moved to a shack at Anderson Creek, right on the edge of a cliff. The highway running through Big Sur had been built by a colony of convicts. We occupied one of the convicts' shacks for $7 a month. There we spent our second year.

Then I met a wonderful woman called Jean Wharton whom I've written about in *Big Sur and the Oranges of Hieronymus Bosch.* She was wonderful to us. She had this house that I now own. One day she said, "You know, this house really belongs to you two people. I can see you living in it. Why don't you take it?" I asked, "With what? You know I have no money." She said, "If you want the house, I'll sell it to you. You can pay whenever you have the means. I'm not worried about that." I agreed and in two months time I got my first big unexpected check from France. I paid for the whole thing right away and $1,000 extra as a bonus.

This is the house on Partington Ridge that "Tropic of Cancer" paid for. In the beginning it consisted of only one room. Over the years, with the aid of my friends, I added a small bedroom, a porch, and eventually a studio larger than the house itself.

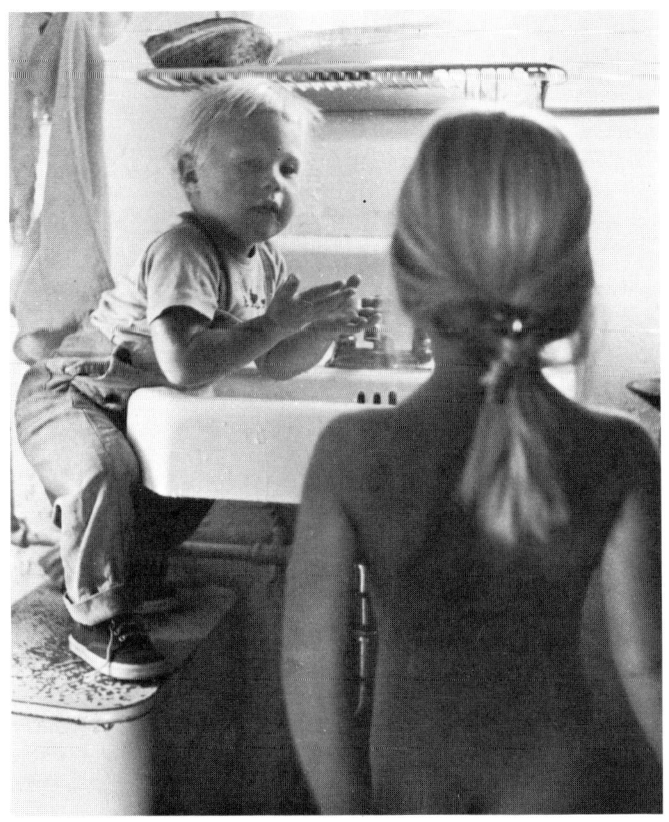

My two children were a blessing. They weren't born at home—we had no conveniences. There was no doctor in Big Sur, not even a telephone nearby. From the time they were born, I was a very happy man.

When my children were very small I used to get up at night to feed them. And much more. I changed their diapers, too. In those days, I didn't have a car; I would take the dirty diapers in a bag, a big laundry bag, and walk six miles to the hot springs (now taken over by Esalen) and wash them in that hot spring water, then carry them home! Six miles! That's *one* thing I remember about babies. For a time, after my wife left me, I was there with the children alone. That's the hardest thing to ask a man to do—take care of tots from three to five years of age, bouncing with energy, and shut up with them in one room, especially during the rains. In the winter when the rains came we were marooned. I fed them, changed their clothes, washed them, told them stories. I didn't do any writing. I couldn't. By noon every day I was exhausted! I'd say, "Let's take a nap." We'd get into bed, the three of us, and then they'd begin scrambling, screaming, fighting with each other. Finally I had to ask my wife to take them. As much as I loved them I couldn't handle the situation. It was something I'll never forget. That experience increased my respect for women, I guess. I realized what a tremendous job women have, married women, cooking meals, doing the laundry, cleaning house, taking care of children, and all that. This is something no man can understand or cope with no matter how hard his work may be.

The kids were fairly close together in age, two and a half years difference. They fought all the time, like sworn enemies. Today, of course they're good friends.

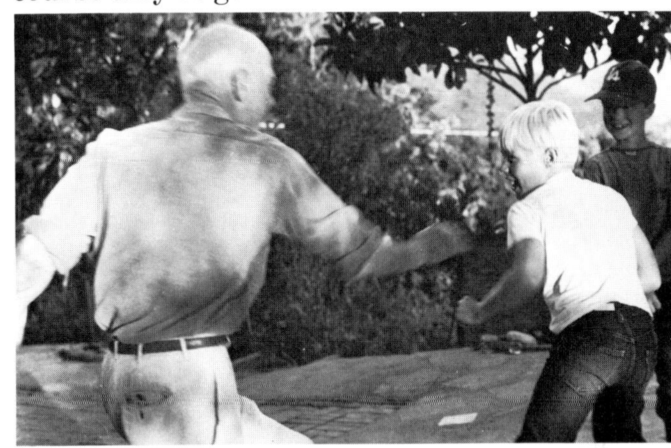

My son Tony and I were very close. I was always at the disposal of my kids when they wanted to play. It was no hardship for me since I like to play as much as children do.

When Val was able to toddle beside me, when she was about three years old, I took her into the forest every day for a long walk beside a narrow stream. I pointed out birds, trees, leaves, rocks, and told her stories. Then I'd pick her up and carry her on my shoulders. I'll never forget the first song I taught her. It was "Yankee Doodle Dandy." What joy, walking and whistling with this kid on my back. Anyone who hasn't had children doesn't know what life is. Yes, they were a great blessing.

At the same time I was having terrible quarrels with my wife. We were most unhappy together. There was a big window in the tiny little studio where I worked. The kids used to come and rap at the window. "Can you come out? Can you come out and play?" My wife had forbidden them to bother me when working. She'd punish them if they did because I wasn't to be disturbed at work, but I welcomed these interruptions. "Sure, what do you want to do? Play ball? Go for a hike?" I'd answer. I think those were my happiest days. For me children are at their best between five and eight years of age. Even younger, it was still good. Not too young, though. They have to be able to walk and talk a bit. At dinner one evening I began a story which never ended. Every night they'd say, "Tell us what's next." And fast, without thinking, I'd continue the story. It was fantastic. I wish I had written it all down. They were spellbound, listening to this daily serial. I didn't think at all. I didn't have time to. It just poured out of me. I had invented a couple of incredible characters, and put them through the ropes, made them do weird, impossible things. Action above all! The best part of it was that I never knew what was coming next.

What came next was the divorce. The usual seven years had gone by and the marriage broke up. Lepska left me.

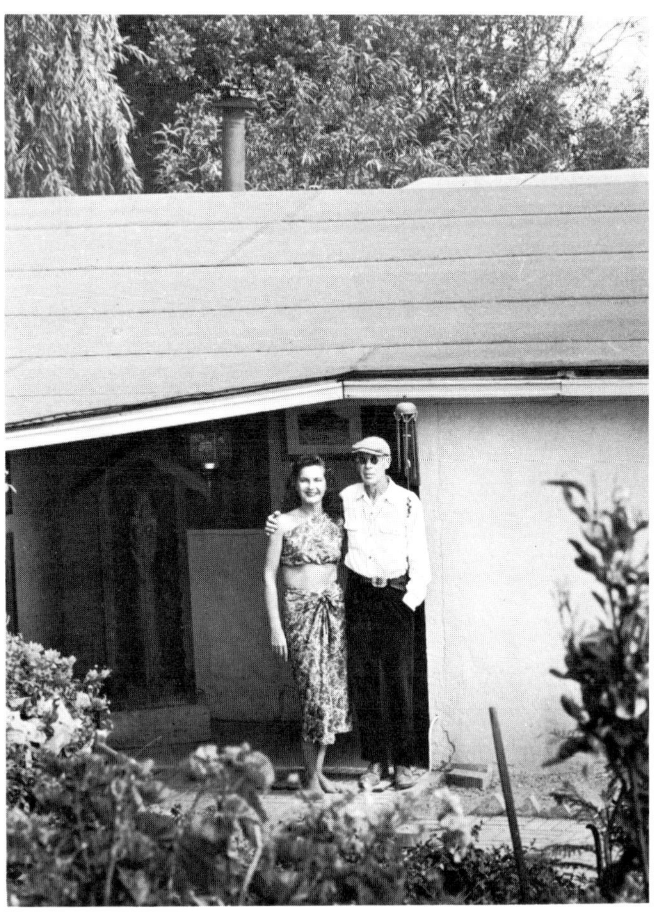

A few months later another woman entered my life. A woman who came out of the blue. She lived in Los Angeles and was an ardent fan of mine. We began to correspond. She knew everything about me and everything I had ever written. I never met her until the day she arrived, saying:—"Here I am." It was on April Fool's Day. I'll never forget! "Here I am to stay, if you want me." That was Eve.

We didn't get married right away. We lived together for seven or eight months and then we took a honeymoon in Paris and married when we returned to Big Sur. She must have been 27 or 28 at the most and I must have been 60 or more. The age difference never bothered me. It never has. I don't think you can draw any specific conclusions about the effect of the difference in age between husbands and wives. It depends on the individual. With a man of a creative nature age doesn't matter greatly. Look at Pablo Casals or Picasso. With younger women you're not only the father again but the teacher and lover too. As for the sex end of it, that again depends on the individuals concerned. I know some marriages where there is very little sex but the relationship is a good one. To be sure, the older man is always at the mercy of a young blade who is good looking and often with no brains. He can usually steal the woman away, away from even the best of men.

Sometimes a woman can go along happily married to a much older man, have a few affairs perhaps, but with no thought of breaking up the marriage. Men don't realize how *much* a woman can disregard that so-called physical attraction, how they fall for homely, ugly, older men sometimes. Jesus, sometimes these homely bastards get the most beautiful women!

People always ask if there's a similarity in the women I marry, and I suppose there must be. Sometimes I am aware of it. *Sometimes.* And yet, if I place one beside the other, they're completely different individuals. One would have to say no, they had nothing in common. But they must have had something in common *for me.* I'll tell you what I think the attraction is. I like strong women. I'm a passive sort of man, weak in a way. You know, I'm not the "he man" type and I'm always attracted to women of strength and character. I've noticed that. My battle with them is a battle of wits. Also, I find that I'm intrigued by women who are devious, who lie, who play games, who baffle me, who keep me on the fence all the time. I seem to enjoy that!

This romantic photo was taken shortly after my marriage to Eve. Several times a day we walked this path to take in the grandeur of mountain and sea, a view which rivals any I have seen in my travels.

It was with Eve that I made my initial return to Paris after the war. As part of her education I introduced her to the great wines.

Back to Big Sur after the Paris trip. We are still in love. In a way we always were in love, even after our divorce.

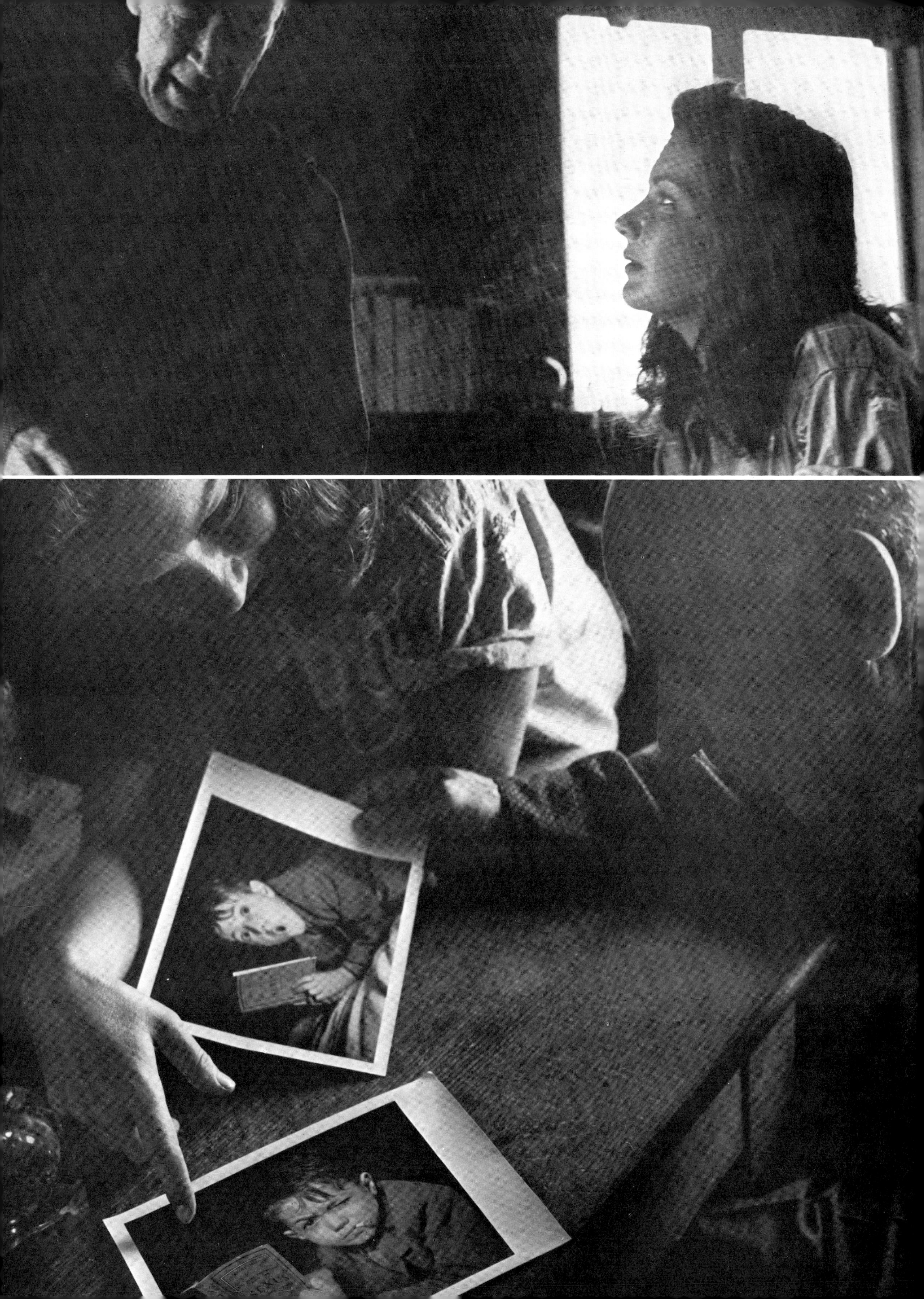

This mosaic representing the signs of the Zodiac was created by my good friend Ephraim Doner. It is embedded in the wall of the studio, an imperishable reminder of my days in Big Sur.

The terrace too is a Doner mosaic. We had no routine chez Miller. We often spent hours doing nothing.

Actually, I have found very great differences, both mentally and physically, although I must say that virtually all the women I loved were beautiful. Most of my friends agreed with me on that. They were sexually attractive. There had to be a sexual attraction, but I was never preoccupied with that aspect. It's the character of the woman, the personality, the soul, you might say, which concerns me. Believe it or not, the soul of woman is what gets me most.

Men always say, "The women *I* select." I say they select *us*. I give myself no credit for selecting. Sure, I ran after them, I struggled, and all that, but I can't say, "Oh, that's gotta be mine. Now that's the type I want and I'm gonna get it." No, it doesn't work that way.

So many men look upon a relationship with a woman from the sexual angle. It's the *thought* of sex that's interesting to me. Everything about it, everything connected with the realm of sex intrigues me. Of course, I have a great imagination. I can wonder and be mystified about how it's done here and there, everywhere, by what variety of types, and so on. But sex isn't an imperative. I can go without too.

I do think women find it difficult to live with me. And yet, you know, I think I'm the easiest person in the world. But it turns out that there is something tyrannical in me. And maybe my critical side comes out very strongly when I live with a person, whether man or woman. I have a great sense of caricature. I discover quickly one's foibles, one's weaknesses, and I exploit them. I can't help it.

That's the kind of person I am. I start out by putting women on a pedestal, by idealizing them, and then I annihilate them. I don't know if what I say is exactly true—but it does seem to work that way. And yet I remain friends with them, all of them except one woman, warm friends. They write me and tell me they love me still, and so on. How do you explain it? They do love me for myself, but they can't live with me.

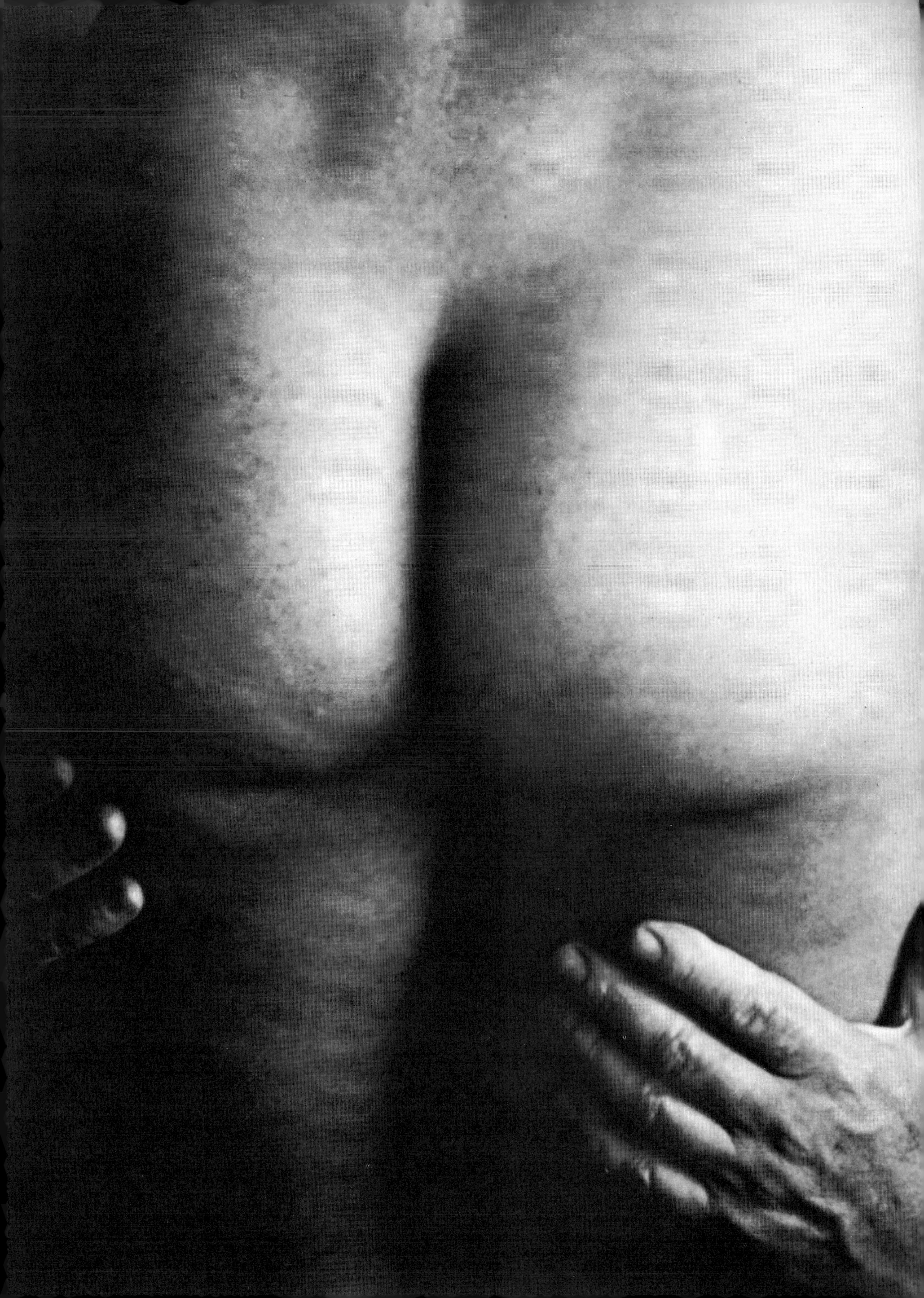

I never had any great trouble writing wherever I was put, perhaps because I only write when I feel like it. I never forced myself. I wrote every day, always from a fresh source. I had discipline. Living in Big Sur, I went to bed early. There was no television, no radio, no nothing. I was in bed at 9:00 and awake at dawn. I'd watch the sun come up. After breakfast, I'd go straight to my study and write until noon. Then I'd take a nap and after that, if I had the energy, I'd paint. And with it all I managed to find time to play with the kids, and take long walks by myself in the hills or the forest.

My principal friend in Big Sur, my great friend, was Emil White, who came a month after I settled there. He was my closest friend and visited me frequently. Or I'd visit him in his shack by the roadside. They were quite different, my conversations with him, than those earlier ones in Paris with Michael Fraenkel. He was easy going, Emil, and always ready to make you a meal. He was a great reader too. He made a meager living selling books by mail order. He had had an adventurous life before coming to America. At the age of 17 he was once sentenced to be executed because of his involvement in the revolutionary movement in Hungary. He escaped by a miracle.

There were a number of interesting people in Big Sur. There was, of course, my nearest neighbor, Harry Dick Ross, whom I saw frequently. He was another great reader and possessed a wonderful library. He was one of the best read men I ever knew. Every year

This is Emil caught in a characteristic pose. I can't imagine why he looks sad. He always loved the feminine touch.

he reread his favorite authors. I spent many wonderful hours talking to him, not only about books but about everything under the sun. Like so many rare characters he was a self-educated man.

Then there was Jack Morgenrath, who came from New York. He was a marvelous fellow who had never lived in the country. He had been brought up to be a rabbi. He came to Big Sur because he wanted to live this wonderful pure life he had heard about. He didn't know what to do when he arrived, but he soon found work as a gardener, going from one house to another. When he stopped in for a glass of wine, he'd stay for hours at a time. We talked about many, many things, including religion and philosophy. He was a gentle, peaceful, anarchistic soul.

Then there was another wonderful fellow whom I saw again on my last visit to Big Sur—Howard Welch, the garbage collector. He was delightful. He came from Missouri. He showed up one day seeking to join the Big Sur community. He said, "I don't know what I can do. I have no talents of any kind, but I'm willing to do anything." So in the beginning he

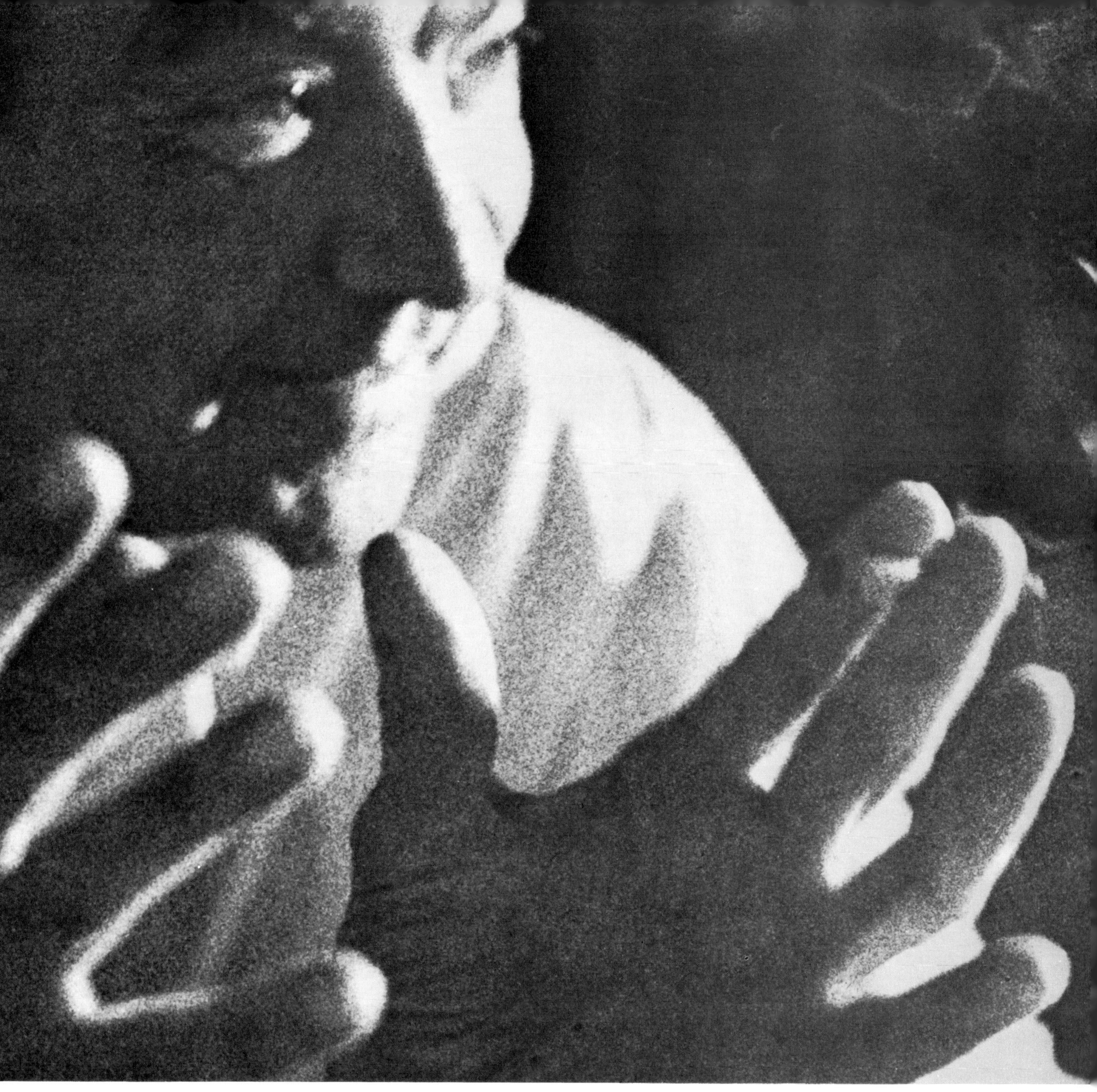

dug ditches, washed dishes, repaired plumbing, all kinds of odd jobs. Then one day he discovered that what we needed was a garbage collector. We were forbidden to throw garbage and refuse in the ocean. We were supposed to haul it to Monterey, forty miles away! So Howard bought himself some huge barrels and a truck—somebody subsidized him—and he collected our rubbish every week, charging us a modest sum for his trouble. He made a very nice living this way. He too had no real schooling, but it was a delight to hear him talk. He would collect the trash, bring it to his home, where he had a big yard, dump it all out and look through it, sort it out, find things, wonderful things that people threw away. His home is made up of these discarded things—beds, chairs, birdcages, everything! This is a man, I want to tell you, who has really made a success of himself. Not moneywise, but spiritually speaking. This man is a happy man. This man is now writing, drawing, painting, and all on his own. He doesn't have grammar, nor does he spell properly, but he writes! I tell him, "Howard, that's wonderful. Don't worry if nothing's published. You enjoy writing?

Then keep it up." He said, "Henry, you're the one who started me on the right path." By that he meant—to do what one likes to do and nothing else. Maybe God disposes of the garbage.

There was one man—I don't know if I mentioned him—whom I knew in the beginning when I first arrived on Partington Ridge. He and I were the only ones living on the ridge then. He lived up at the top. I was only a thousand feet up. His name was Jaime Di Angulo, whose father had been ambassador to France from Spain. Jaime had run away from Paris at about the age of 19 to become a cowboy in America. He became a cowboy. Then he lived with the Indians, and was made a Shaman. He studied to be an anthropologist, and later to be a physician, at Johns Hopkins. He was a man fluent in many languages. He had a crude cabin up above. Before coming to Big Sur he had lived in San Francisco in grand style. When he came to Big Sur he adopted a totally new way of life. He lived like a savage, sometimes roaming about stark naked. He rode horseback a great deal, often naked. In the center of the cement house that he had built for himself, he had a big chopping block. A few feet away was a table loaded with dictionaries in foreign languages. He wrote a book on language which was never published because it was too unorthodox. He hunted for his food—and cooked it in the open fireplace. He had made a hole in the roof to let the smoke out. He had a tragic death.

I had a friend in Carmel Highlands named Ephraim Doner who was a painter—a great individual. On my way home from shopping in Monterey I would stop by his place and have

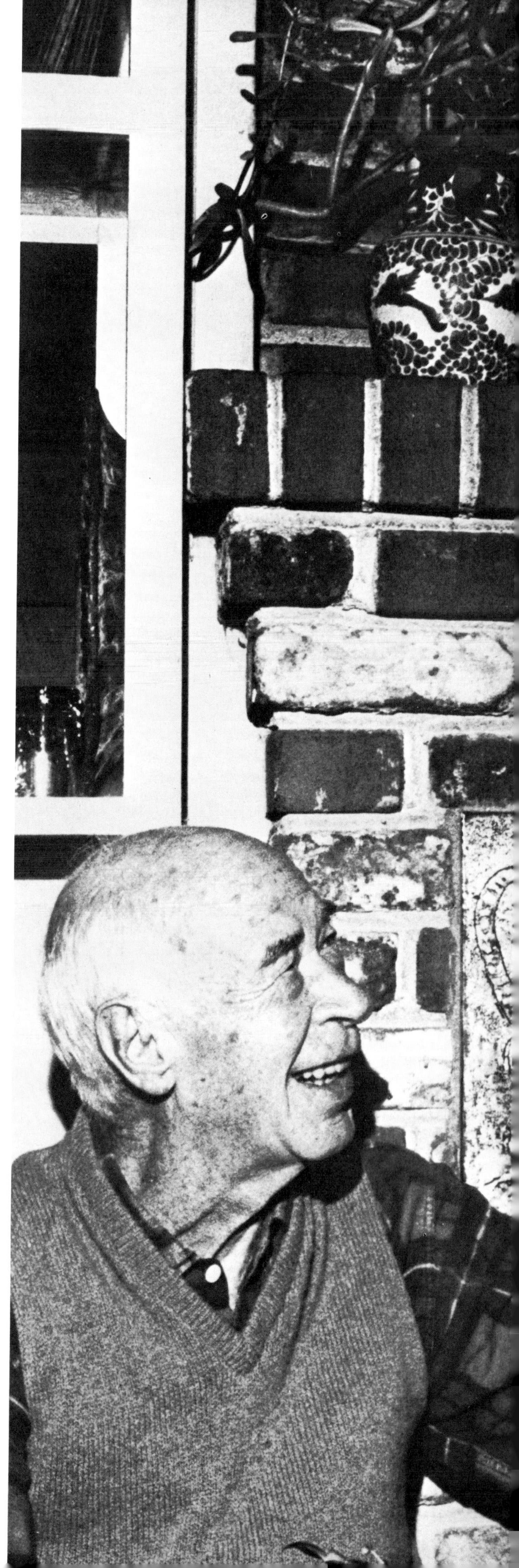

At the home of the painter, Ephraim Doner in Carmel Heights, California last year. Every day he becomes more and more like a figure from the old testament. His life and art are one —a blessing and a benediction to one and all.

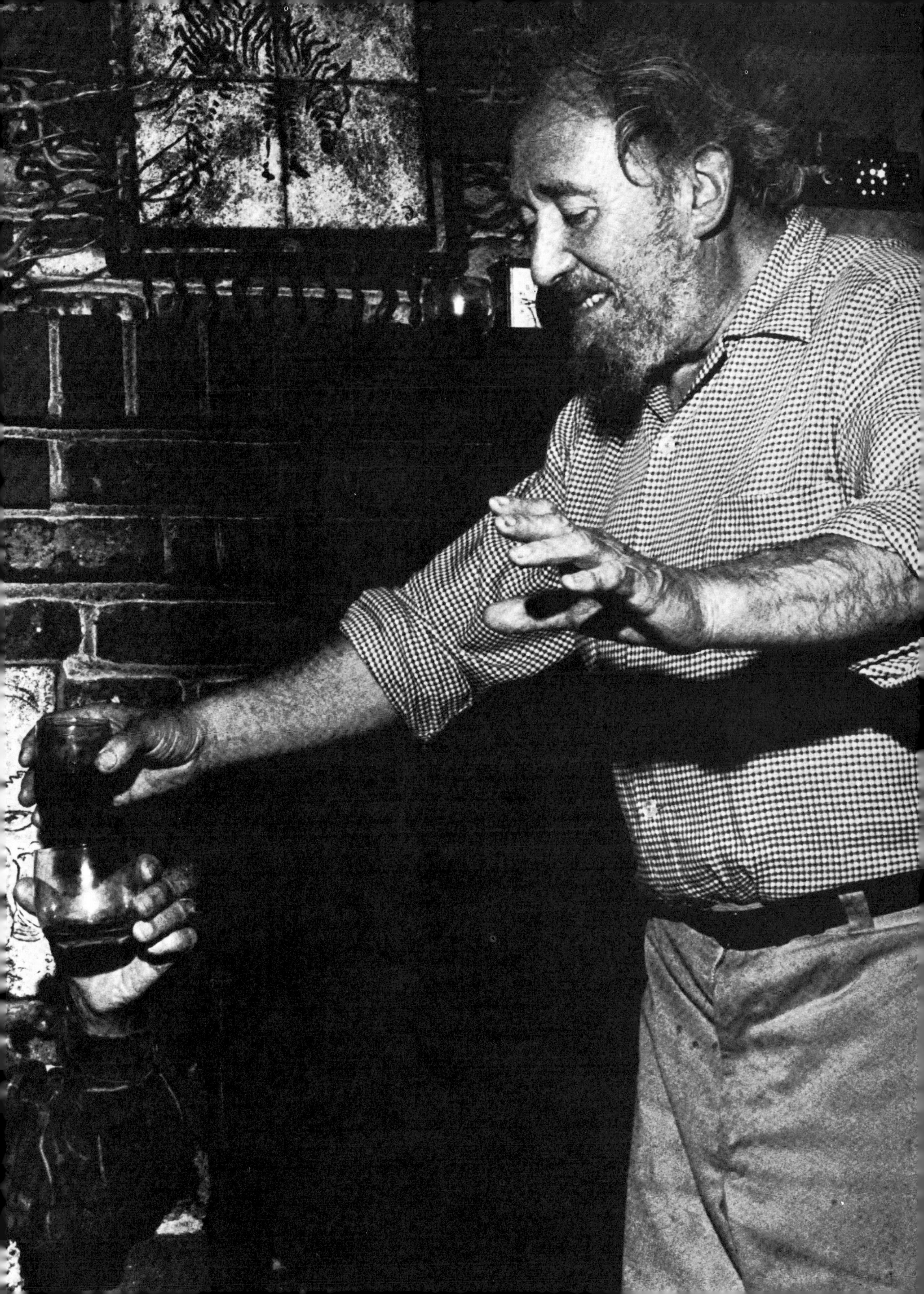

dinner with him. He was a great cook. We also played ping pong a great deal. Doner was very poor. He never made any money to speak of. Yet on my way into town he would be waiting for me at the gas station to see if I had enough money to buy groceries. If he was broke he'd borrow from the service station man to help me out. A wonderful friend!

Six months after my arrival when people began to know that I was living there, I had a steady stream of visitors. They came from all over the world, I must say. High and low, good and bad, every kind of character barged in. Often I was out in the yard doing heavy work when a visitor would arrive. I'd explain that I didn't have time for him, but if he insisted on talking to me, he could pick up a shovel or hoe and help me. And they would do it.

Today Esalen Institute has taken over what was originally Slade's Hot Springs. Nude bathing at these Hot Springs is not a new idea. I used to soak myself regularly along with the other members of my family in an old tub.

NOTICE TO VISITORS

The undersigned wishes to inform all and sundry that he has long since left the Abode of Peace, that he no longer has any comfort or inspiration to offer, and that even the migratory birds avoid this spot. Prayers are offered up daily, — without charge. The garden has been transformed into an open air Vespasienne. Look toward Nepenthe when you water the flowers. If you are seeking Truth travel a little farther south: you will find it at Ojai chez Krishnamurti. Be kind to the children — they abide. For a metaphysical treat stop at the Big Sur Inn which is also a haven for stray cats and dogs. Life along the South Coast is just a bed of roses, with a few thorns and nettles interspersed. The life class meets every Monday regardless. Refreshments are served when demanded. Those interested in celestial navigation are advised to first obtain a rudimentary knowledge of integral calculus, phlebotomy, astral physics and related subjects. The use of liquor is strictly forbidden on interplanetary flights.

When you come please be so kind as to check your neuroses and psychoses at the gate. Gossip may be exchanged during the wee hours of the morning when the gremlins have left. Please bear in mind that this is a small community and news travels fast. (Carrier pigeons are provided when necessary.) Fans and other obnoxious pests would do well to maintain silence. Questions relating to work-in-progress will be answered in stereotype fashion in the columns of the Big Sur Guide at the usual space rates. God is Love — and in the ultimate Love will prevail. Remember, man is the ruler, not Saturn! Let us do our best, even if it gets us nowhere. In the midst of darkness there is light. "I am the light of the world," said Jesus. He said a mouthful. Light, more light!

Respectfully,

Henry Miller

I never make any pretense of doing something I can't do well. All of my carpenter work was done through visiting friends. I can't drive a nail in straight. I am no carpenter at all. I was fortunate in having good friends all my life; if I am unable to do things I have friends who can and who enjoy helping me.

Though I did not do any building there was certainly enough other work to be done keeping the place free of brush. We always had to clear the brush. Don't forget that when I first arrived there the place was literally a jungle. The poison oak was as high as the ceiling of this room, and covered about half an acre, the biggest patch, that is. With the help of a friend, I managed to clear most of it away. About a year later I undertook to dig up the whole garden about an acre in size. I dug deep trenches, like in World War I, in order to get at the roots of the poison oak. It was a futile job because the roots are seemingly endless. I was always cutting things down. Even when I walked down the road to get the mail I had an implement in my hand and I would chop away all the hanging brush as I walked along. It was the only way to keep the trail clear. But I did no building and I laid no tiles. The tiles were laid by my friend Doner. Living in Big Sur was rigorous. I had to be in top physical shape. It was a most active life. For the first year or two I walked up and down that hill every day, a distance of two miles each way. A long steep hill. I not only fetched but I also carried packs full of things on my back—groceries and kerosene for the lamps, all sorts of things. I often had to make two trips to collect all the stuff. Then, every day after I had finished work, I would take a walk in the hills. That would be another four or five mile jaunt. When the children were little, one of them was always on my back or on my shoulders.

I made one big trip to Europe with Eve shortly after she arrived, and then another with someone else which contributed to my leaving Big Sur.

You see, when married I did not run around with other women. There have always been plenty of women in my life but these escapades, if I may call them that, usually occurred in those periods when I was not married. As I said above, toward the end, when I was invited to be a judge at the Cannes film festival, I asked a young woman in Big Sur to join me there. Eve had said she didn't mind. But the very day the girl arrived in Cannes I received a cablegram from Eve saying, "I'm getting a divorce."

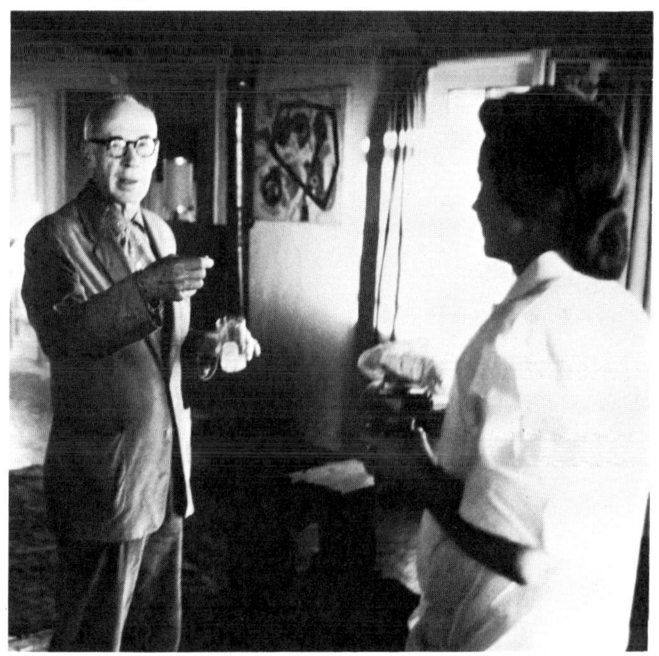

Every day of my life at Big Sur I had before me the incomparable vista of the Pacific. Its ever-changing aspects offered me alternately peace and stimulation. I had to learn to live with this overwhelming force which is hidden within its obvious grandeur.

When I returned from Europe I continued to live with Eve for a time. It was a bit difficult, as you can imagine, living with her after the divorce, even though we remained good friends. During this time the children were living in Los Angeles with their mother who had married and divorced again. The children begged me to come and join them and establish a family again. They missed me and I missed them, so I agreed to do it. Eve remained in Big Sur and shortly after that married my next door neighbor.

I found freedom in Paris and I found peace of soul in Big Sur. I think I really became totally integrated there.

On a recent visit to Big Sur I found no radical changes—just a few more houses and a few more people. Big Sur remains much as it always was. It seemed unspoiled to me. And I think it always will be that way.

But I wouldn't go back there to live. That part of my life is over with. Once I leave a place, I leave it for good. Besides, I couldn't support that life any more, physically. Too much up and down hill for my arthritic hip. But it was so wonderful when I went there last December, with the rain and everything. God, the moment I got there, I asked myself, how could I ever have left such a place. The air was so invigorating, the horizon endless. Standing on my terrace facing the vast ocean, I always thought of China thousands of miles away and of the world to come, a world of peace perhaps.

When I left Big Sur to live in Pacific Palisades Emil was the last to bid me good-bye. Do I regret having left Big Sur? Frankly, I have never regretted anything. Regret, like guilt, is a waste of time.

The thing is to become a master and in your old age to acquire the courage to do what children did when they knew nothing.

PAINTING

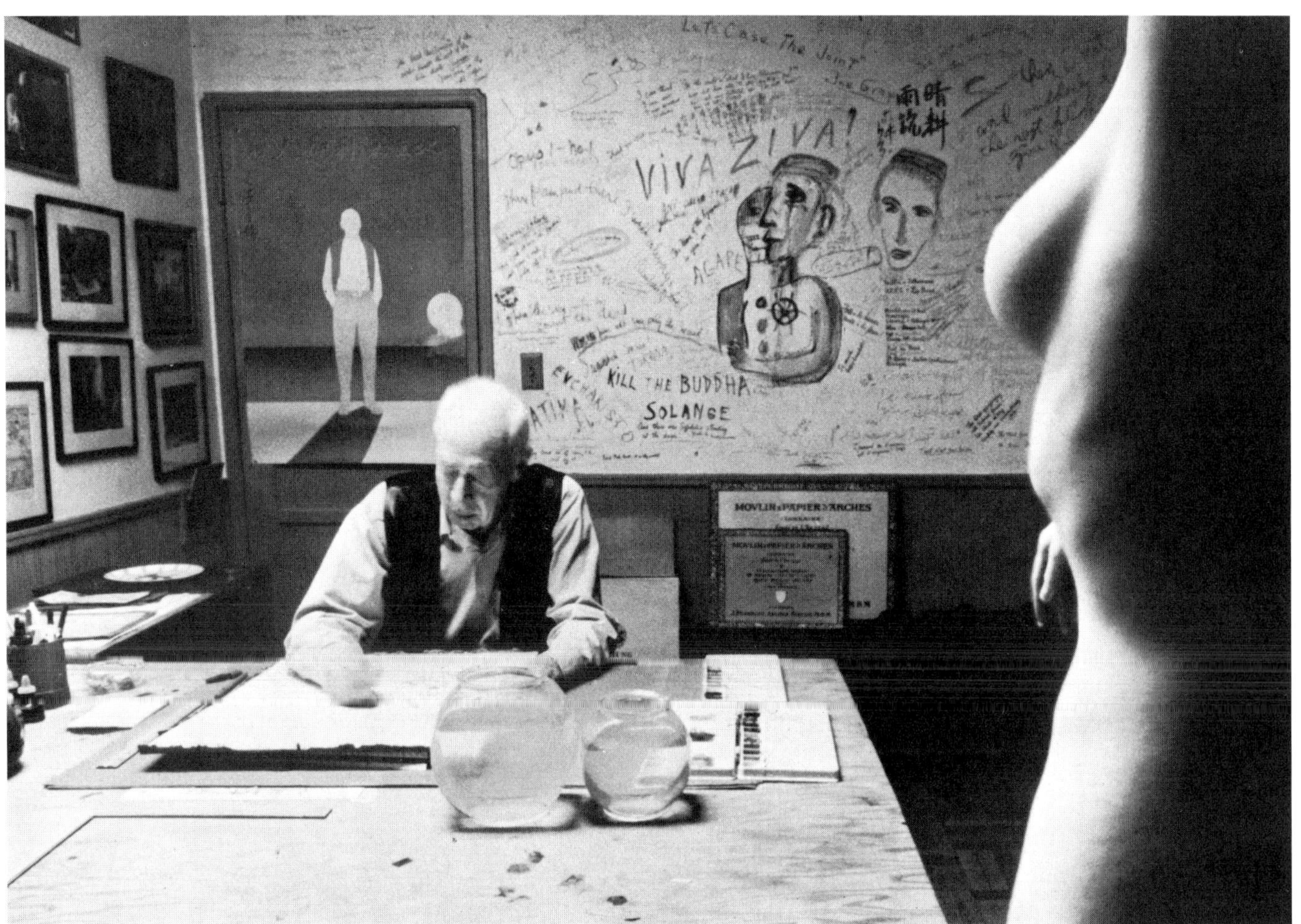

In this small room I do all my painting. My friends and visitors have helped decorate the walls. The portrait of me as "the Brooklyn Boy" in the background is by the Japanese artist Yokoo.

My description of painting is that one is looking for something. I think all creative work is like that. In music you sound a note. That leads to the next note. One thing determines the next. When you come down to it, philosophically, the idea is that you live from moment to moment. In doing so each moment determines the next. You should not be five steps ahead, only the very next one, and if you can keep to that you're always all right. People think too far ahead, with detours and all that. Think only about what comes next. Do only what is right under your nose. It's such a simple thing but few people seem able to do it.

You have no idea, I suppose, how I first began to paint. I had a boyhood friend who remained my friend up until a few years ago when he died. I knew him from the age of ten. The difference between us was that at ten he was already a talented artist. The teacher would say, "Go to the blackboard, Emil, and draw us something," and he would. Unfortunately, at an early age my friend became a commercial artist. He had to support a mother, father, sister and brother. He never became a great artist but he was a great lover of art. We spent whole nights together looking at books on art, studying reproductions, discussing styles, periods, techniques. This was a very important period in my life. I had not yet done a thing. I felt I had no talent for drawing or painting.

Henry miller
36/65

Henry Miller
9/48

For Hoki – a princess from the Far East
Henry Miller
5/9/65

ANNO D'AMARE
Henry Miller
51 | 66

Henry Miller - 1/67

Henry Miller
64/64

La Mère Ubu
Henry Miller

The change came about through looking at an album of George Grosz's watercolors. The cover of this album (Ecce Homo) had on it the portrait of a man. One night, I don't know whatever possessed me, I copied this portrait and I copied it very well. I said, "By God, maybe I *can* draw and paint." And so I began.

So much went on in those early days when I first took up the brush. That was a period when I was desperately poor. All I could do to amuse myself was to get paper to paint on—any kind of paper, wrapping paper, butcher's paper, which is wonderful for certain things, you know.

But let's not forget my friend Emil who provided such a wonderful background for me, who gave me the feeling and the reverence for art. Emil Schnellock of Brooklyn. He had the talent but he ended up a failure as an artist. He became an art professor in a girls' college. He was a good teacher, that I must say.

Later I worked with a few artist friends of mine—Abe Rattner, Hilaire Hiler, Hans Reichel. I told them I wanted to learn more about technique. After two or three lessons they said, "Henry, stop it. Don't try to learn. You're better off without it." They all discouraged me, but in a kind way. They meant that they didn't want to kill what little talent I had. Also, they recognized that I'm hopeless at learning. And they were so right.

The painter I revered most was Hans Reichel, a German artist exiled in Paris. I liked his work even more than Paul Klee's. Paul Klee and John Marin are the two watercolorists whom I would like to be able to come somewhere near in my work but I never do. And if I could say who influenced me, they, along with Reichel, would surely be foremost. But first of all before them, long before I heard of them, were the Japanese artists. I still refer to them today as my beloved artists and idols. I mean artists like Utamaro, Hiroshige and Hokusai. I never tire of looking at their work.

People are always saying to me, "I see you changed your style in this one." I say they don't know what they are talking about. When you think that I have done 3,000 watercolors by now, and I have a pretty good idea of what I did, I simply don't know what people mean when they make such remarks. My style changes, certainly. I change from day to day, but it isn't a radical change as with a Picasso because I do not have his ability.

I sometimes feel sorry for Picasso although I know he is one of the great, great men in this world of ours. But I feel sorry that he is the slave or victim of his creation, that he's a compulsive artist. They say he's not happy unless he's working. He can't enjoy not working, as it were. But I must say one thing about him. To me everything he says has high wisdom, and it's said beautifully and with wit. You can ask him about anything, even things he doesn't know about, and you get a wonderful answer. Because that mind of his is turning over all the time, and it isn't a mind that says, "I've been trained, I know, I've studied." No, it's a quick spontaneous sort of thinking. You see, I think that there are very few real thinkers in the world, that we are all sleepwalkers; we are not thinking, we are reacting all the time. We are telling what we heard, what we have borrowed from others. We have no thoughts of our own. But Picasso says things with originality and, even if they're crazy, lopsided, topsy-turvy, it makes high sense to me.

And now I come back to another thing, why I love the Chinese and their wisdom. Because to the Chinese all this thinking and creating is just a game. There is no ultimate significance to it. It's the best game there is perhaps, but it's only a game. Painting is a game to me. I only know that I want to paint; I don't know anything more than that really. I like the feel of the brush in my hand. But what it is that I am about to paint, what happens, I never know.

Sometimes I look at a postcard or an advertisement and it sets me off. "I'd like to do something like that," I say to myself. Picture postcards really excite me. I put the card down in front of me and tell myself I'm going to copy it. It may be a scene of a harbor with boats and buildings; of course it turns out quite different under my hand because I am incapable even of copying well.

In this water color I was trying to imitate de Kooning—without much success.

There was a time when I associated certain countries with certain colors. Like China—I remember—yellow, yellow. The Chinese yellow was always something that intrigued me very much. I used to spend whole days or evenings with Emil Schnellock, my first painter friend. We often talked about colors. I once asked him, "How do you make gold?" Yes, I would ask naive questions like that. It would go on for the whole night, this talk about gold, how to make it, who did it best, and so on. For a week or more I would be crazy about yellow, thinking only yellow, painting yellow.

By the way, I often make use of the sponge. It's very effective in watercolor now and then. Another thing I like very much, where I am most successful perhaps, is when I have made a failure. It's usually a very good sheet of paper which I don't like to waste. So I take the watercolor to the pool and scrub it as much as I can. No matter how much I wash away there are still traces left. Then I turn the faded painting around and I paint something entirely different over it. The faint background of the failure makes the picture.

There is a philosophical aspect to this sort of technique, something I feel people don't ever realize. The one great power we have is our ability to transmute things. When a thing goes wrong you have to turn the wrong into the right. This is the one thing God gave us, I feel, and this is the greatest thing about the universe—that it can be altered. It's capable of any transmutations whatever. Man has a bit of this power in him: to take what is lost and failed and convert it into a new and wonderful thing.

It happens very often that I paint two figures. It is sometimes difficult to determine which one is male and which female. Many times when I finish a figure I ask myself is it male or female? It doesn't matter. I will make what I think is a man's head and then give the figure breasts because I am not concerned about whom they belong to. Sometimes the breasts are just interesting in themselves.

I am always searching. The more I look at George Grosz' work the more I marvel and wonder at his use of color together with his draftsmanship. He can take big patches, orange, black, gray, any colors, and blend them with lines which interweave in dexterous fashion. This I consider real skill, real knowledge. He was a master. His early works were brutal and they were meant to be that: a condemnation of the German nation, the people, the whole people, condemned forever. I don't think that even Goya has done to the Spaniards what Grosz has done to the Germans. He left an indelible mark on them. They are condemned for all eternity in his paintings. And yet it's an aesthetic treat, however horrible and brutal the subject matter.

There is no satire in my paintings but I do use a variety of symbols. And I repeat them, I know. Certain symbols recur time and again. One is the Star of David, and if you asked me why I couldn't tell you. The moon also occurs frequently, a half moon or a crescent moon. I think that's because it's a decorative thing. But I don't have any *reason* for using a symbol. In fact, I don't have any reason for doing anything. That's the interesting and strange thing; that's why it's difficult to talk or write about my painting. When I sit down to paint I seldom know what I'm about to do. Sometimes I have a rough idea; maybe I would like to do a landscape, but the landscape may turn into something quite different as I go along.

I've always preferred Jewish holidays to Christian ones. On Yom Kippur and Rosh Hoshanah I use traditional Hebrew symbols in my water colors. The words add another dimension.

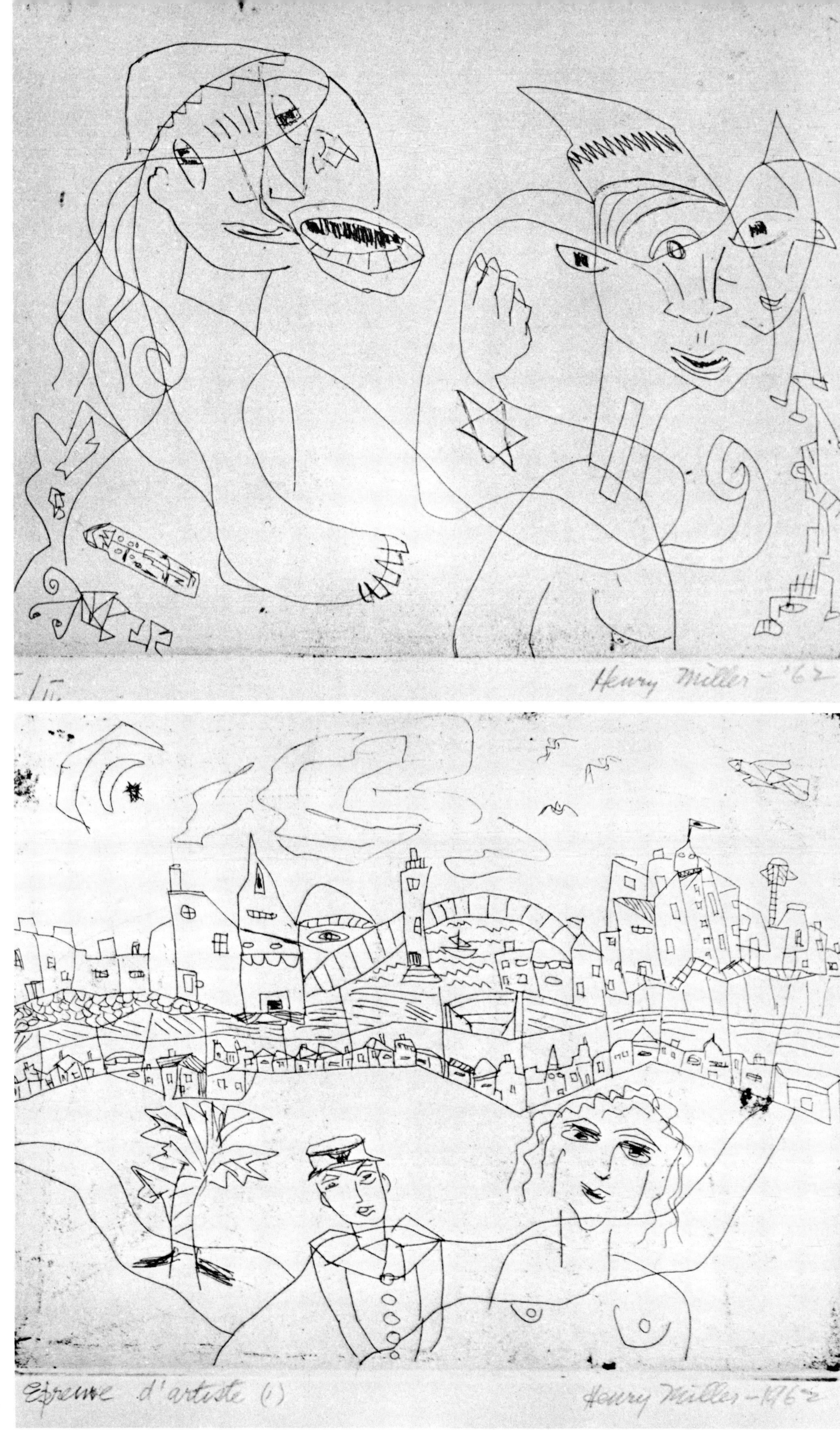
Henry Miller – '62
Epreuve d'artiste (1)
Henry Miller – 1962

More and more I have found that the proper way for me, not for everybody but for me who was not born a painter, had no talent and is still lacking in a great many things, is to follow my instinct, let the brush in my hand decide what I am going to do.

With writing it's the same. I try not to think. I try to uncover whatever is inside me begging to be revealed.

There are all kinds of paintings and of course there are different schools. They have definite ideas which they follow. One follows this trend, another that, but I don't have any trend. I've got skids under me. Each picture is a new adventure.

Astrological signs are very powerful symbols and they have significance for me, but I'm too lazy to consult them or copy them. So out of my head I do something that reminds me of an astrological sign. Sometimes they are quite wonderful. Of course all symbols are exciting. In my mind the only true and lasting language is the symbolic language. The language of words by which we communicate is a very limited one. Symbolic language is permanent, indelible.

I paint fish often because they are easy for me. I don't try to do something I can't do. An artist looking at one of my paintings with a fish in it may say, "You know, that's really out of place there." Who's to say? I can swear that I never had a feeling about why I wanted a fish in a picture. These things come to me automatically. Something else might have done just as well. Such things don't bother me. What does bother me often is people saying that I paint like Marc Chagall. I admire Marc Chagall. I admire him a lot but I have never thought of imitating him. It does not take much of a critic to see the difference between me and Chagall.

I'm a great admirer of Ucello too, and Seurat. I wish I had the time and the ability to do large detailed canvases like Seurat. I have so many great favorites, including a few of the old masters. There are other masters, like Leonardo de Vinci whose work means nothing to me.

Sometimes I like to color the paper beforehand. I may lay down several washes, not just blue or red. I used to work out a beautiful background before beginning to paint whatever. If the paper was still moist, so much the better. I liked what happened when the paint got blurry, when it exploded softly.

I can also tell you another thing you wouldn't suspect. A lot depends on how much time I have. I used to begin painting my watercolors about an hour before dinner, just when the light was fading. Sometimes I don't want the electric light on. I look at my watch. I've got 20 minutes, or 15 minutes, or half an hour. That decides how I will paint.

Usually I'm in a hurry and I want it bold and quick. I have turned out some very good paintings in ten or twelve minutes. It's really amazing because they are often the better ones, I think. Always, too, the better ones come when I'm tired and I think I'm finished, can't do another one. Then I'll say to myself, "Oh, I'll try one more!" And that's the lucky one. When you have all the time in the world and the right paper and you have arranged everything to suit you, you can't paint.

The way I use color in my paintings is often accidental. There's a certain harmony about the colors I put together but I don't really think about it in advance. I don't always know how to lay one color against another. I had the good fortune or misfortune to live with several artists who did know about color. They were rabid on the subject. But I could never quite follow them.

During a romantic interlude at the Berlin home of Germany's most glamorous publisher, Renate Gerhardt, I produced ten etchings.

The painters who manipulate color well are children. Children are reckless and spontaneous when they paint. They express what they feel. And this goes against all rules, in a sense. But it works, it's successful. The older you get the more you realize that children have it. The thing is to become a master and in your old age to acquire the courage to do what children did when they knew nothing.

To lay green on green, blue on blue, that's always very effective. If you went to an art school you would be told all these things. You would know all these things in advance, what you can do and what you can't. Then you have to forget everything you are told. The job of discovering things for yourself is far better than learning it in school. That's why I am against schools in general.

I tried not to send my children to school when I was in Big Sur but the authorities would not permit it. I believe all schools are destructive. They kill curiosity and the desire to learn. All artists are killed in school. As soon as children get out of kindergarten the brainwashing begins. I think you're better off finding out what you need by yourself. Why waste time on learning? Most people who want to be artists are not artists and they are going to drop by the wayside anyhow. So why not begin the hard way? Going to school gives the illusion that knowledge is what makes an artist. It's like knowing how to write English perfectly. It has very little relation to the art of writing.

What am I? Am I supposed to be a critic? I am not, especially of my own work. I don't know what to relate my work to when I look at it. The primary thing for me is simply the pleasure of picking up the brush and seeing what happens. That's another thing, that expression, "what happens." Rather than

planning and delivering and executing I let things happen. If there's to be any judgment about my work, or criticism or appreciation, it has to be done by the viewer, not by the doer. The doer is finished with it the moment he has done it.

Naturally there are certain paintings that I am more attached to than others. Some I regret I gave away. Some I would like to keep just for the pleasure of looking at them. One can say that some paintings are more realized than others. Viewers want to find meaning in everything. They want to see something they are looking for. They are not satisfied to take the painting for what it is, not try and name it, define it, analyze it.

People say that in many of my paintings the faces more or less resemble my own. This is true because I don't know how to draw a face in many different ways. Sometimes I think I would like to do a face showing this or that expression but I don't know how to make these expressions.

I remember trying to do a city floating in the atmosphere in one of my paintings, but I don't think it came through. Those are the kind of thoughts that occupy me. It's often a technical matter with me. How, say, to give the sense of floating or how to make a watery one, for instance. Most things I never seem able to do again. If I knew I would be capable of rendering much more than I do. Do you remember that wonderful thing Hokusai said when he was 65? I quoted it in the beginning of one of my books. He said that at 65 he was just beginning to learn how, and he had been painting since he was a young man. At 65 he was getting a hint of it all. At 75 he might be able to do a little better and when 100 he thought he would be able to do most anything. At 100 mind you. And he actually lived to be almost 100.

People have said that I look at my own work more critically than most artists do. Sometimes I have the audacity to look critically at the work of the masters. You know frankly what I think? Ninety percent of what is called the works of the old masters could be thrown on the junk heap. The same for books. I have the same feeling about them. Very little that man has done in the period which is called civilization, which is only some few thousand years old, is of any value to me.

Most people, knowing that I am not a painter but a writer, think what a lot of fun I must have painting because it's obvious I don't care what I do. I don't know enough about painting to execute a thought, an idea, that would express my rebellion against society.

I don't know why I use certain figures at all.

Maybe just to fill in space. People say to me all the time, "Isn't that this or that?" "I see this or that." I say, "That's what *you* see, not *me*." There is a great difference between seeing and looking. People are only seeing with their eyes but they are not looking with their minds, and true sight is of the mind. We wouldn't see unless the mind was working.

There are times when people look at my work and say, "How come we don't see any pornographic, obscene things in your paintings? Why is that?" I don't know why. It never occurs to me when I'm painting. I don't paint from a standpoint of ideas. I express my ideas in writing. Painting is a day by day spontaneous thing. Whatever comes out comes out.

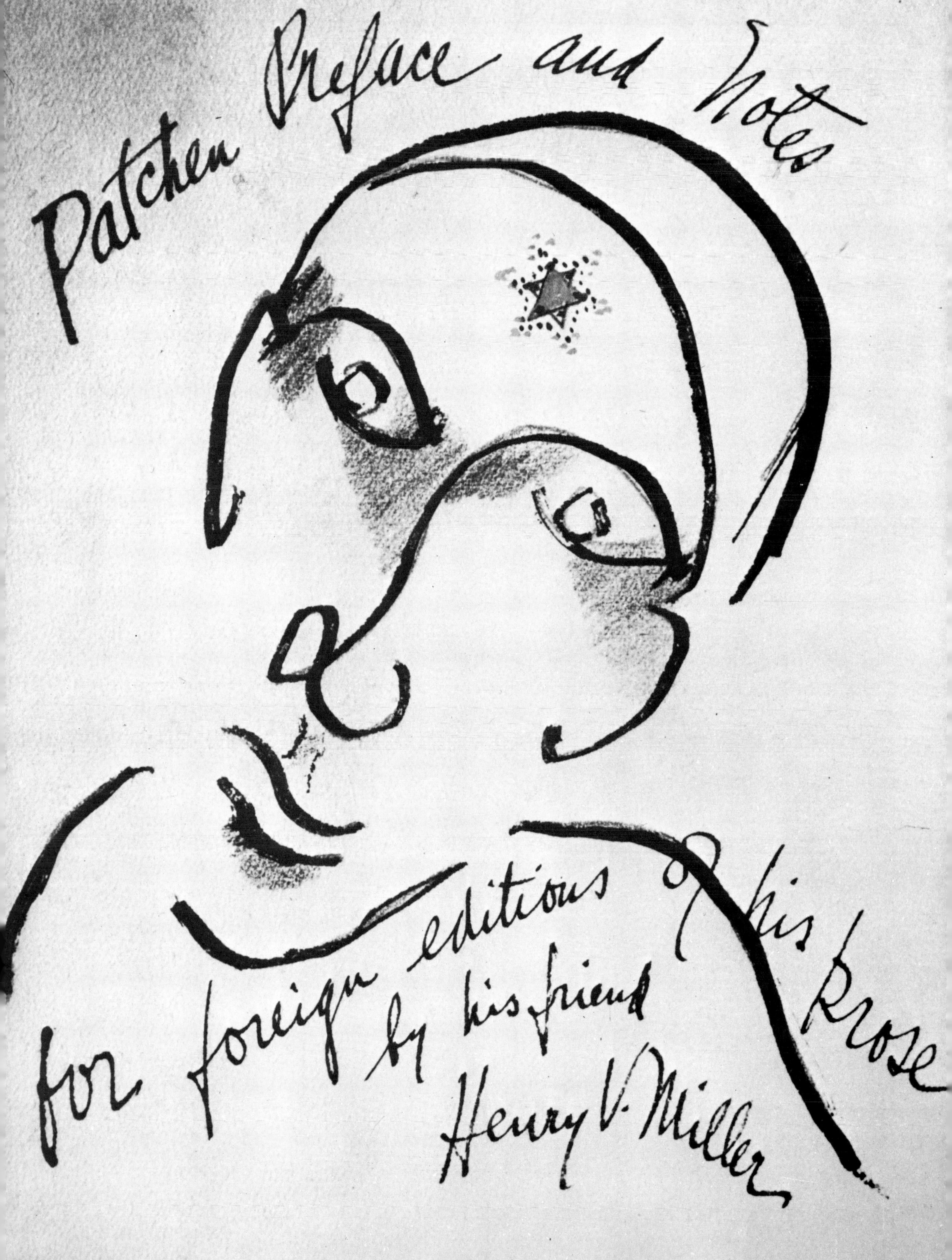

Patchen Preface and Notes

for foreign editions of his Prose

by his friend

Henry V. Miller

Henry Miller 11/63

Henry Miller 4/68
For Jack and Millie

1967
Henry Miller

For Kuba and
Henry Miller

For Hoki-San
Henry Miller
3/7/66

Henry Miller
24/66

Henry Miller

WAWANA
50
NIPPON
KANUNİ SULTAN SÜLEYMAN
1496-1566 / 400. YILI
5
For Hoki-Sama
Pour la bien-aimée
Henry Miller
4/8/66
KRAUT
Raté
M
SONNENAUFGANG
VERBOTEN
GÖTTINEN
Schmutzig
MATERLINK
SCHMETTERLINK
KREBSEN
Henry Miller
9/15/66
Insomnia #4

Nothing matters to me just so long as it works. That's what I say about science. I don't believe in it, by the way. To me ninety percent of science is bogus, yet the other ten percent works. But so does magic! And it works equally well in living as well as in working. I think one of the sad things about life is that everyone is planning ahead, trying to make himself secure, trying to be successful instead of letting the magic take over. Do this, do that, instead of letting "it" take over, whatever the magic "it" is. Let "it" decide for you because I think "it" knows better than you or I. The question should not be, "Is it true? Is it going to last?" but, "Does it work?" And so it is with painting. I found it to be true with writing too, because I often violated the rules and in so doing wrote my best passages.

I don't feel that science and magic are analogous. They are at opposite poles. Magic has existed from the earliest times. Science is only from yesterday. Yesterday could be 2,000 years ago or 10,000 years ago. Years don't mean much. I have to beg pardon for sounding like a professor. I know nothing about these things. But these are my instinctive reactions. I'm the enemy of the scientist and I think he is our enemy *per se*.

Finally, I must tell you something about myself which explains many things. No man is as full of chaos as I am. People think I am an orderly man. My house is orderly and my work table is orderly. But inside I'm a raging chaos. I don't think I could be creative if I weren't so chaotic. Just lately some scholars dug up an ancient manuscript relating to pre-Biblical times. It had to do with the first words in Genesis about the creation of the world. In this manuscript God was said to have brought order out of chaos. This is quite different from creation. What God did was to bring about order. In other words He did *not* create.

That's the definition in my mind of an artist, that he is only a man who rearranges things. Arthur Rimbaud said, "No man ever created anything." Man is not a creator. All man does is turn things about, rearrange things, that's all. That's creation as far as man goes.

For me sex wasn't
an every day thing.
Attached to the woman's
cunt was always the
woman herself. The
woman was the most
interesting thing.

PARIS

I made my first trip to Paris two years before I went there to stay. I was there first with my wife, June, in 1928. We had enough money to last us almost a year. Then we weren't in the destitute condition that I later found myself in. I do remember very vividly my first impression of Paris. We arrived by boat at Le Havre, then took a train arriving at the Gare St. Lazare in Paris. The Gare itself was exciting to me with its glassed-in roof and the big waiting room called *La Salle de Pas Perdus*, "The Hall of Lost Footsteps." It was a very busy place—we had arrived at the evening rush hour – and I couldn't take it all in at once. I was completely bewildered. And I didn't speak any French. Not a word! I knew how to say yes, no, and thank you, but that was all.

How we got the money to live on for that year in Europe is a long story. June, my new wife, was helping in every way to enable me to become a writer. When I failed to sell my work —short stories and prose poems that I had had printed myself – she sold them for me in the cafés in Greenwich Village and on Second Avenue. She met many men during the course of those days; one of them was a man who was very, very fond of her and probably old enough to be her father. She pretended to him that she was a writer, but of course, it was *my* manuscripts she showed him. I was then writing a novel and she would show him pages from it. "Remarkable," he would say. "You sound like a man. You have great promise!" Because he never really believed that she would ever complete the novel he promised that if she did finish it he would give her enough money to go to Europe for a year on her own. He didn't know anything about me, of course. And lo and behold, I finished the novel, and she gave it to him, and we got the money for the trip. It was one of those books that was never published. I think it was called *Crazy Cock*.

In those days our lives centered around Greenwich Village and the East Side, especially Second Avenue, where all the foreign cafés were. When the manuscripts failed to sell, we decided to peddle imported candies, which I carried about in a valise. First, *I* tried selling them. I hardly ever made a sale and was the butt of everyone's jokes. Then June, who was a very good-looking woman, took over and of course she made a big success of it. We would sell $50 to $100 worth of candy a night sometimes.

Then we got this money to go to Europe. Of course, the man who gave it to June didn't know that *I* was going along too. He was a married man and had a business, so that even if he had wanted to go with her he couldn't.

I would think we might have had $1,500 to $2,000 at the most, not more. That included the fare. We went by boat, on a French liner – a famous little boat – which was the flagship of the French fleet at that time.

We left Paris after a few weeks and decided we were going to travel all over Europe. We bought bicycles and I taught June to ride. We cycled from Paris to Marseilles where June met with an accident that ended the cycling. Sometimes we'd take a train, go a short distance, and then ride along the tow paths of the canals. For lunch we'd buy a hunk of salami, some French bread, cheese and fruit, and eat picnic fashion. It was beautiful and cost next to nothing.

I remember where we lived when we first arrived in Paris. We stayed at the Grand Hotel de la France on the Rue Bonaparte, right near the Beaux Arts. I didn't know any French, but I had a pocket dictionary. One day, when we were out of cash, my wife suggested that I go see the hotel owner and ask her if she would lend us some dough. I looked in the dictionary and instead of saying, "Could you *lend* me some money," I said, "Could I lend *you* some money!" The *patrone* laughed and said, "Of course!" but I got the loan.

Notes on ~~Joan.~~ June

Destructiveness: clothes, towels, shoes, socks, hats, expensive gowns, worn to shreds in no time, or ruined by cigarette holes, by spillt wine or gravy, or paint. Habit of doing what she likes regardless of what she has on--because it would cramp her style. Allowing others to wear her things and ruin them for her: fur coat, beautiful slippers, evening wraps, mantillasm searves, etc. Mislaying, losing, having things stolen: purses, bracelets, pendants, costly kerchiefs, gloves, money. (Finding 50 dollar bills floating around on floor, staircase, in clothes closet, etc. where they had fallen out of bag in which they are usually carried all crumpled up, like used toilet paper. Hence super-cautiousness on my part in guarding own personal belongings which have a special personal value for me. Dictionary, for instnace, watching it each time Joan uses it so that it will not be dropped on floor, or leaves wrinklled, or pages cut out or torn. (Giving as excuse, sometimes, the fact that it is still unpaid for.) Traits such as this often observed in kept women who have never had to struggle to earn a living. (Emerging from theatre or restaurant with hat full of sawdust or plaster from floor or walls. Indifference!

Money matters: always, everywhere, no matter under what circumstances ~~,~~ we live, an accumulation of debts with tradespeople, friends, etc. Living always into the future, big plans for big coups, with only ridicule for saving, caution solid effort, etc. (All this petty, narrow, bourgeois, futile.) In order to liquidate small annoying debts gets involved in larger ones because of some scheme, a panacea, that will solve all financial problems.

Forbidden fruits: enchantment~~s~~ which drugs, vice, eccentricity, anti-social acts (murder, thievery, incest, etc.) have for both Vanya and Joan. Always a contempt for the normal, the sane, the thorough-~~gin~~ going, the respectable. (also Richard, the homo following her like a puppy) Mother & daughter in love with each other, then falling in love with June and having jealous scenes. As witnessed by the degenerate Italian dope fiend

Roman name, June Edwards, Ebba Foote, Phyllis

All saying they could fall in love with her if she were not a woman!

A year later, when I arrived alone, I was very, very poor. I was always waiting for June to send me something. The first restaurant I picked to eat at, on a wonderful little street, right off the Place St. Sulpice, was a very modest one called "Le Gourmet." The food was good and it cost something like 27¢ a meal. That included wine and dessert. You had a napkin with a napkin ring that you'd put in the box after you finished; the napkins were changed once a week. After I ate there a couple of weeks I knew that I was going to be up against it sooner or later. I said to the woman, the owner, "If I were in need," — I don't know how I managed to learn all that but I learned fast — "would you give me credit? Could I still eat here?" And she said, "Yes, of course," just like that. And a few weeks later I asked for credit and I got it. I must have eaten there for two months and they never asked me for money. It was remarkable. That was Paris in 1930.

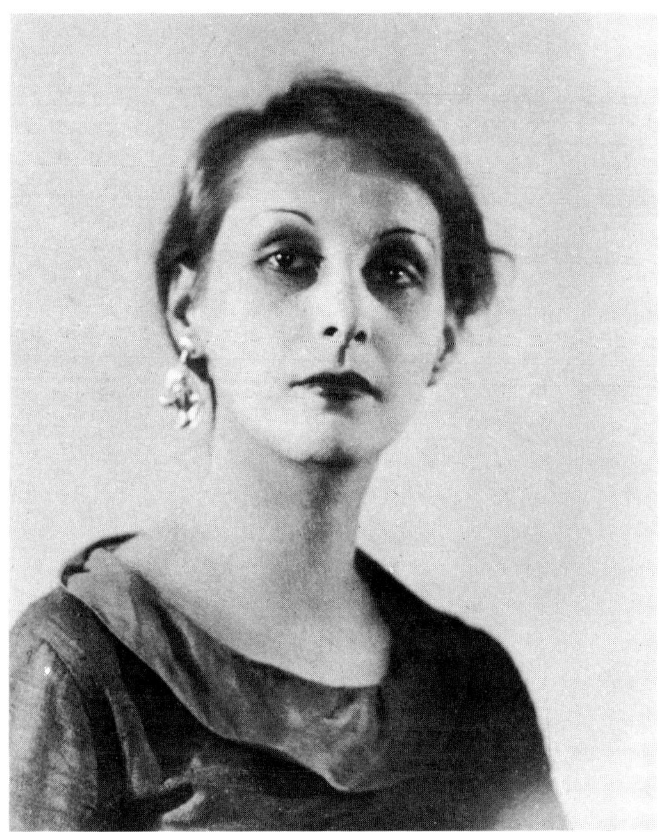

June was then in New York and sending money to me when she could. She worked at all sorts of things. I never knew what she did to get the money and I didn't inquire too closely. She sent me money as long as she could but it didn't last very long. She somehow couldn't make it anymore and I was stuck. Then came those terrible days when I'd get up every morning to look for a "friendly face," someone who would buy me a meal, someone who would put me up for the night, because I couldn't afford a hotel anymore.

I didn't think much about "tail" then. Food and a place to sleep were more important. It was a nightmare. That went on well over a year.

Then I bumped into a fellow at the American Club one day who said that I resembled his old scout master. He was a lawyer, a very young man, and a would-be writer. He was a Yale graduate. He treated me like a father. When he heard that I was down and out, he took me to live with him in his apartment. I used to cook for him at night. I remember the big, blazing stove, snow on the window panes — a huge studio it was. I took care of the flat, made the fire, and had everything nice and ready for him when he came home from work.

I could cook in those days. I wasn't a great cook but I could make a meal with most anything. I'd make stews very often.

I lived with him for four or five months and I was writing all the time, even in the beginning. Of course, I wasn't writing books at that time. I was writing letters that were the basis of my books, you might say. I wrote letters to one good friend back home, the painter who had inspired me to start painting, Emil Schnellock. There's a book of my letters to him now coming out. I would describe every day what happened to me — what I discovered about Paris. A lot of this material is in the *Tropic of Cancer*.

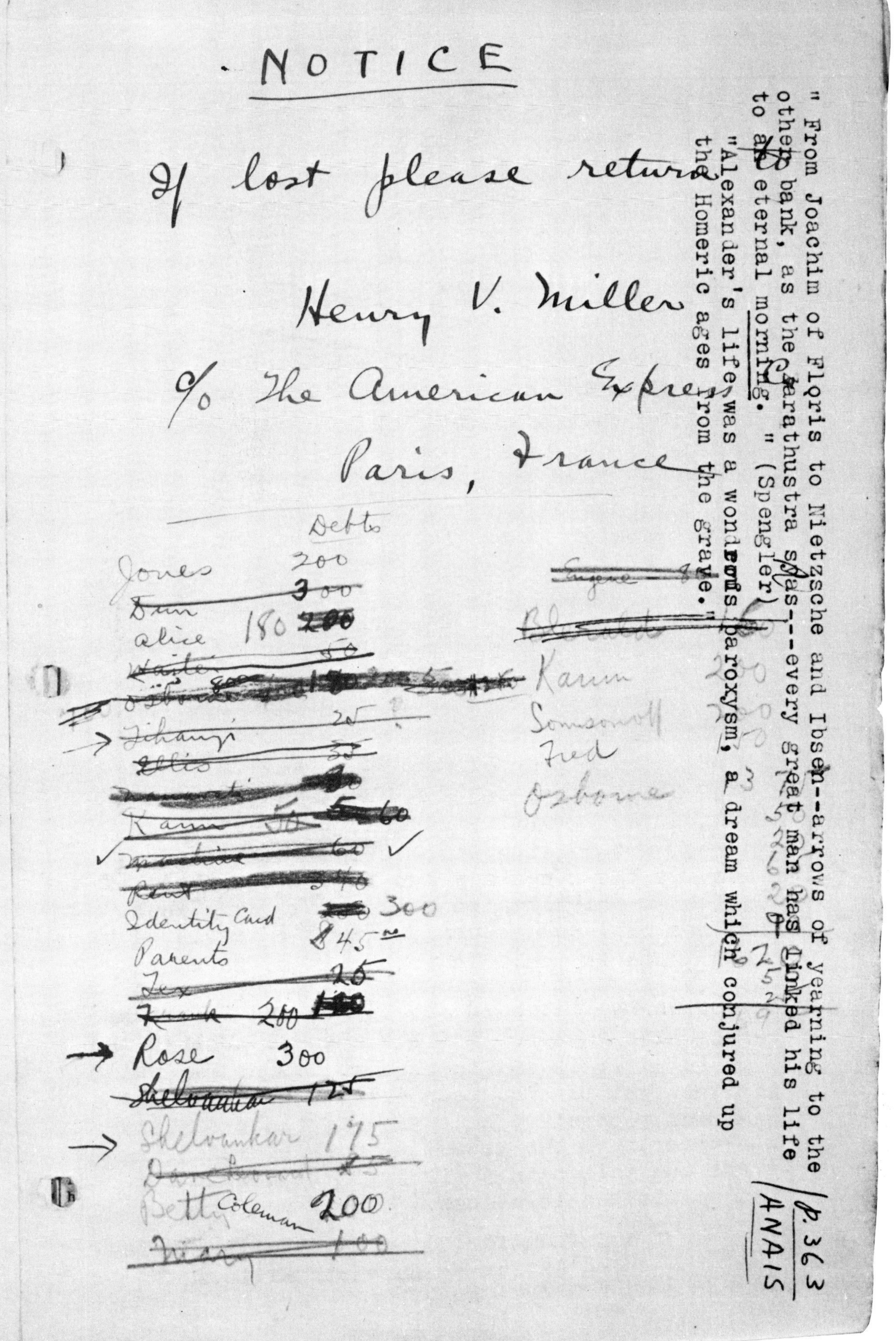

NOTICE
If lost please return
Henry V. Miller
c/o The American Express
Paris, France
Debts
Jones 200
Rose 300
Shelvankar 175
Betty Coleman 200
Karun
Somsonoff
Fred
Osborne
" From Joachim of Floris to Nietzsche and Ibsen--arrows of yearning to the other bank, as the Zarathustra says--every great man has linked his life to an eternal morning. " (Spengler)
"Alexander's life was a wondrous paroxysm, a dream which conjured up the Homeric ages from the grave."
p. 363
ANAIS

This is one of the many notebooks I kept from the time I began to write and beg and borrow from all and sundry. Eventually—maybe 30 years too late—I paid off all my creditors who were alive.

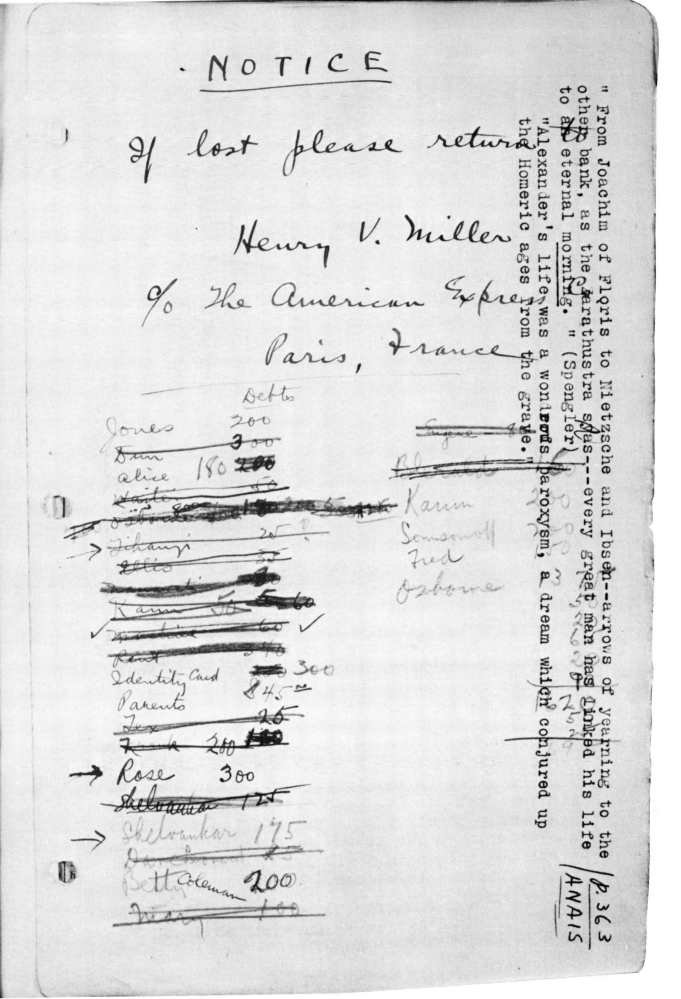

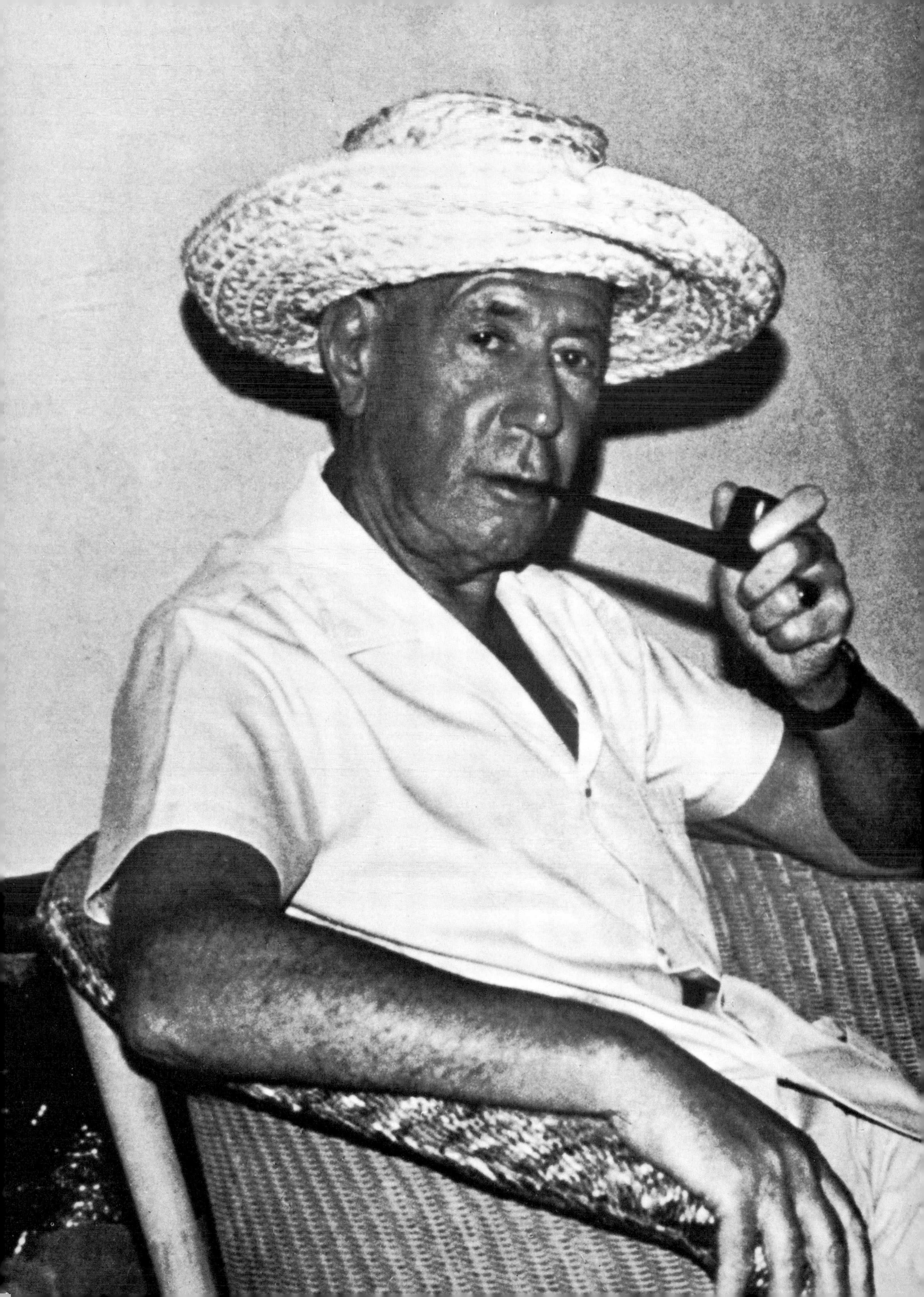

Then I met Alfred Perlès who became my bosom companion for the whole time I lived in Paris. Fred lived in a hotel, a very cheap hotel, and I used to wait for him to finish work. He'd finish about 2:00 in the morning. I'd wait for him at a café and then go home with him to his hotel. This was in the days when to enter a hotel, the cheap ones, you'd press a button and the door would spring open. You'd have to call out your name and room number as you passed the concierge's window. As Fred shouted his name I'd be tiptoeing right behind him, traveling lightly on the balls of my feet so the night porter wouldn't hear me. Then I'd have to sleep in bed with Fred. Imagine!

In the morning, when he left for work, Fred would leave money on the mantelpiece for me for breakfast. I would have to pretend that I had just visited him if someone came. This went on until he got me a job on the *Chicago Tribune* as a proofreader. The pay was little. Usually we'd blow the whole week's pay on a good meal and a movie in one night.

We finally decided to rent a small apartment in the suburbs, outside of Paris – Clichy was the name of the place. I later wrote a small book about this episode – *Quiet Days in Clichy.* A movie has now been made from it. After a time we managed to buy two bikes. Saturdays and Sundays we would explore the countryside.

We spent a lot of time hanging around the cafés, like the Dôme, the Select, the Rotonde and so on. When we were broke we would consult the incoming boat schedules. There were always college girls, young American broads, coming to Paris on vacation. We learned how to cultivate them. They would buy us meals and lend us money. In addition we'd get a free lay now and then.

Here is Alfred Perles my boon companion of the Paris years. Sitting in his room in Cyprus, he hardly looks a day older today than when I first met him at the Cafe du Dome, Paris, in 1928. His motto and always was, "Easy does it."

Women . . . there were always plenty of whores. They were pretty inexpensive then. I would say that they are about twenty times more expensive today. The same for rooms. Think of it—the room that Perlès had lived in — a miserable joint, no bath, toilet in the hall, and so on — well, if I'm not mistaken, it cost $3.50 or $4.00 a week. Today, when I go back to a similar hotel, do you know what they charge? About $10 a day. *A day!*

There were always plenty of whores about, some of whom came to be good friends with us. There was one called Mademoiselle Claude whom I wrote a story about. She was rather exceptional. Germaine, whom I write about in *Tropic of Cancer*, she really didn't mean anything to me. During the period when I was working on the *Chicago Tribune* as a proofreader there was a little bistro nearby where we ate after work. The back room was just big enough for a dozen or so clients. We knocked off work at about 2:00 in the morning, the hour when the whores were quitting work to join their *maqueraux*.

In the back room of this bistro we all met and ate together. I remember the Algerian girl with the great big eyes, a beautiful looking whore, who was also very well-read. She used to talk with me about Proust, Paul Valéry, André Gide, and such. She knew their work intimately.

One night on her night off, I happen to meet up with her. It was my night off too. It's a bar in Montmarte. I see that she's dead drunk. I like this girl and I don't want anything to happen to her, so I suggest that I take her home. Just a few blocks away, right in front of a famous whore house, a very well known one run by two English women, she decides she has to take a leak. She squats down right there in front of the place and lets out a stream that ran into the gutter. The next thing I know she's taking a shit. Then a cop comes along and threatens to haul us in. Somehow I managed to talk him out of it. I decided to put her in a taxi and send her home. She was weeping like a cow.

I don't remember ever having the clap in Paris, but I did suffer badly from the piles. I didn't get rid of that problem until years later when I met a wonderful proctologist in Berkeley. After a few visits he said to me, "You know, I don't think you have to worry any more about this. If you have a recurrence, don't let it worry you. Don't think about it. It will pass away. Above all, try not to worry." I took his advice to heart and I never suffered again from that ailment.

As I said before, my boon companion in those days was Alfred Perlès. He was at my place almost every day to see me and often I had to feed him. I could cook for five or six people, if necessary. If there were a few girls for dinner we always managed to have some excellent wines on hand. Often we would be drunk by the time the meal was over. Perlès was a bit of a clown. One night when he was drunk one of the girls dared him to take his clothes off. No sooner said then done. As he danced and cavorted, he knocked glasses on the floor. By this time, he was reeling. Then he begins to imitate Hitler which he could do very well. As he prances about he slips and falls on the broken glass. Soon he's bleeding from head to foot. Everyone is laughing, including Perlès who by now is a gory mess. When the girls left I put him on the couch in the studio. During the night he fell off the couch. In the wee hours of the dawn he found himself lying in a pool of blood and vomit. He was still laughing when he picked himself up to go to the bathroom.

Life today is so different.

Mlle. Claude was a charming prostitute from the Touraine region with whom I fell in love for a time and wrote about in my first published story in Samuel Putnam's "New Review."

Paul Morand's "New York" 67

p.218 Jews: "Et pas de Juifs! s'écrie ce peuple égalitaire. A mesure que l'Europe abat ses barrières sociales, l'Amérique élève les siennes. Les préjugés de race s'y accroissent d'année en année, bien que les Américains aiment peu à s'expliquer là-dessus et que la presse n'en souffle mot... Des immeubles achetés par des Juifs déclassent un quartier."

Gave Mlle Claude all but this page of my notes on "New York" together with the book which was the first French book I tackled. Used to read it in the Hotel St. Germain-des-Pres before retiring.

Exchanged for a good lay!

2.

typewriter is all I lack, and to-day I am going to make an effort to induce one of the firms here in Dijon to send to Paris for a machine. Should I fail I will write you, enclose the necessary money and ask you to try to arrange it from the other end. (The rental is usually 60 frs. a month.) To-day also I go "for a walk" with the head professor of English, and I am going to ask him if he can aid me in getting private pupils. They tell me he is a good scout, despite his severity, his 'sadistic' turns in the class-room.

Perhaps I sounded like a cry-baby. What a yawp I set up! Damn it, I wasn't supposed to fall into a bed of roses. So, if in the future, I rave or rant, just set it down to literary ebullience. Everything has its compensations.

When I took the job to teach English at the Lycée Carnot in Dijon I didn't realize that I would only get room and board—no pay. One of my fantasies was that the school would provide me with a typewriter. Of course they didn't.

Typical idiotic letter from Madeleine. And she has never returned the MSS.

7.

resentative
idley, Paris
uin, Paris
tz, - Berlin

Madeleine Boyd

48 East 49th Street
New York City

Telephon
Wickersham 2
Cable Add
Bravboyd, New

January 14, 1932.

Mr. Henry V. Miller,
Hotel Central,
Paris.

Dear Henry Miller:

I am still sending your things around. They are so good I think there is a chance of their being sold. When I finally do give up hope of selling them I will return them to you.

Your last letter was very amusing and I would have answered it but I was in the country at the time recuperating from an automobile accident.

George Buzby came in to see me today and enjoyed reading your letter. I see Betty Salemme Occasionally.

Very sincerely,

Madeleine Boyd

Joe – add her to our list of "half-wits"!

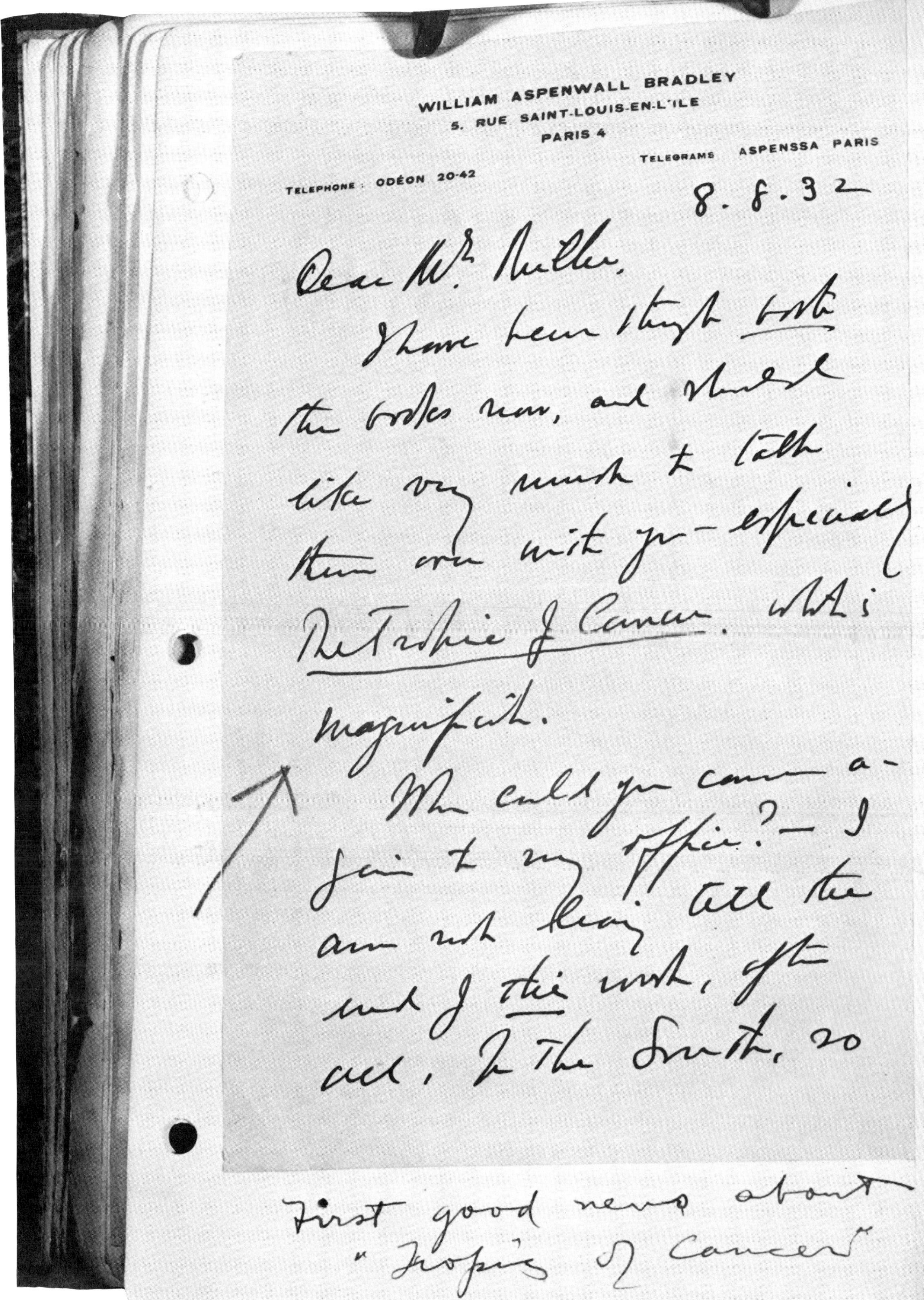

WILLIAM ASPENWALL BRADLEY
5, RUE SAINT-LOUIS-EN-L'ILE
PARIS 4

TELEPHONE: ODÉON 20-42

TELEGRAMS ASPENSSA PARIS

8.8.32

Dear Mr. Miller,

I have been through both the books now, and should like very much to talk them over with you—especially The Tropic of Cancer, which is magnificent.

When could you come again to my office?—I am not leaving till the end of this week, after all. To the South, so

First good news about "Tropic of Cancer"

I don't know whatever led me to William A. Bradley, a literary agent. The day I delivered the manuscript to him turned out to be one of the luckiest days of my life.

Tropic of Cancer --Insert. 3.

Purity of obscenity when it reaches boiling point of violence and rage. Wal
in Levallois-Perret, everything coming clear..Above all no piety, no reverenc
Lost on B'way, adding up lights, zero in crowds, everybody reducing everybody
to nothingness, all overawed and squashed by products we built--lights, buildings, bridges, etc. Burlesque, restoration to self, accent on body, smut for
own sake, religion of carnality, oodles of flesh, Margie Pennetti and Cleo
(see MSS. on this for Izzy the gallery god scene, for picture of ghetto, etc.)
Swinging doors Blvd. La Chapelle, rue de la Goutte d'Or and re d e la Char-
bonniere (Irene)--impreszson in early evening, whores at doors with cigarettes
calling to passersby-red glow. Thinking of Cocteau's feeble drug dreams, his
feeble homosexuality, his feeble brilliancy, etc.--prefer Goya's stuffed dolls,
skeletons in lace, etc. to women of Lawrence & Gide. Osborn's mantic talk,
his volcanic flow, his having something even if enfeebled, etc. Zest and gusto
for life, which a Zadkine couldn't see, which Paula ridiculed, which Nichols
alone made something of. His New England winter scenes, his Dickens' Christ
mas feeling, his Cemetery reminiscences, ancestral theme, old age, grandmoth
in wheel-chair dominating family circle, father bringing him into world alon
His relish for Wilke, Shngai, L e Havre, white whales, Melville, Conrad--ig
norance of danger, self-obssesssion, whole drama with Jeanne very interesting
and hideous and last letter reveals worlds on this subject. Mss. lost or
scattered--containing worlds--good as Rimbaud or Velaine. Why did no one per-
ceive what I had, except Ronald Miller? Stick the arm in up to eyes and
waggle them ferociously--crazy, metallurgical eyes, nonsense, monster. Thoughts
when June says "you're a saint...you're the most honest person...Jeanne theme."
And then about the mystery-- "you're not a great person, I would never explain"
Effect of this now. Steel walled. Untouchable, unassailable--Proust after Al-
bertine's death, and pages on sorrow and retrospection, etc. Elsa Von Bernburg.
Several refrains to repeat--"fucked out cunt" , "poor tired ass", "sorry for self

I have told all about how and where I lived in Paris in *Tropic of Cancer*. I lived from street to street, hotel to hotel, one studio to another, from day to day. I had no regular address. I got up in the morning, always without any money in my pocket, walked down to the Boulevard de Montparnasse, passed the Dôme, the Select, the Rotonde, looking, as I always say, for a friendly face. I got to be like a criminal, reading faces. Is *he* my meal ticket? Is *he* the guy who'll help me? I could size people up pretty well. Usually the ones who helped me were American or English, now and then Russian. Rarely a Frenchman.

I'd find myself telling all kinds of lies, which never bothered me, to be sure. Even to this day I can lie, if need be, and think nothing of it. I consider certain lies as white lies. A lie that isn't intended to do any harm, a lie that enables you to preserve yourself in an emergency, I think is justifiable. No, I never had any feelings of guilt about that. Certainly I told many tall stories, all kinds. When you think back to those days that were so crucial, in which your life hung by a thread, you no longer remember what you did and said precisely, because it happened at the moment, was spontaneous and sincere. Even if it was a lie, it was real. It gets washed out in your memory. I never had any particular line. I never was a man who developed a line. I always acted intuitively, instinctively.

I became acquainted, I don't remember how, with a very celebrated agent in Paris. He was himself a celebrated writer, William Aspenwall Bradley. I had first shown him another book which he didn't think much of — one I had written in America. And then I showed him this new one — the *Tropic of Cancer* — and he was immediately fired by it. He said that there was only one man in the whole world who would dare to publish it and that was Jack Kahane who owned the Obelisk Press. Jack Kahane came from Birmingham, England. He had lived in Paris for many years and had made it his home. He published mostly pornographic books, most of which he wrote himself under a pseudonym. Now and then he published some good writers, like Joyce for example. When Bradley brought him the *Tropic of Cancer* manuscript, he knew he had something. He immediately showed it to his French friends, writers and critics, for their appraisal. Everyone was steamed up about it but no one believed it was possible to publish it. Everyone thought it too daring, even for France. It took him two to three years before he finally decided to risk publication. It was Anais Nin who furnished the money for the first printing.

While awaiting publication, Kahane suggested that I write a short book about D. H. Lawrence. I had never thought of writing such a book, though I was greatly interested in Lawrence's work. It was Kahane's idea that my second book should be of a different nature, something to establish me as a literary figure. I protested strongly. Then he said "Well, you could certainly write a hundred pages on Lawrence, your great favorite, couldn't you?" Grudgingly I said yes. And that set me to work doing research. After making voluminous notes, I wrote about 800 pages and quit. I couldn't finish the job. I was thoroughly confused.

I've often said that France provided the climate I needed as a writer. What I have not said is that my inspiration to write was the beautiful and talented Anaïs Nin whom I first met when she was, like myself, unknown. Now she is known throughout the world for her novels and for the successive volumes of her Diary. Over the years we have inspired one another—but my debt to her is greater than hers to me.

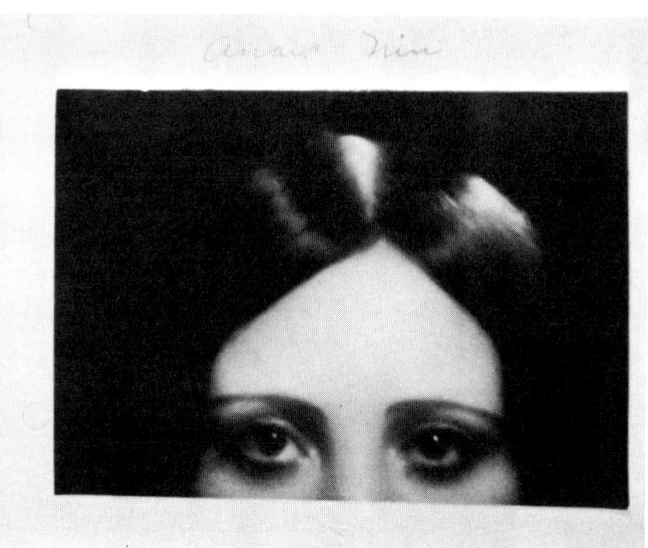

I think I felt even then that Lawrence and I were quite different in our approach to life. To me it seemed that Lawrence made sex too important. Anyway, that little commission to do 100 pages or so was my undoing. I never dreamed I would walk into a labyrinth from which there was no escape. I got so engrossed in Lawrence's ideas that I didn't know any more which were his and which mine. I found him to be full of contradictions, like myself. I was so obsessed that I couldn't stop making notes, night and day. I had a pad for notes with me all the time. In the restaurant I'd write on the paper tablecloth.

This never happened to me before and rarely since. The experience taught me something about myself. One part of me is the writer of tales and another part of me is the man who gets electrified by ideas – and also gets derailed. In this Lawrence work I ended up by saying the very opposite of what I said in the beginning. I was totally confused, nevertheless I wrote some very good finished chapters. I doubt if I'll ever again try to write about a man's life and work.

I think of sex as a very natural thing, like birth or death. I don't think it has to be given special consideration as a subject. It's a big part of life – the half of life, if you like, but I don't see that we need put such great emphasis on it. Lawrence did, however. It was a big thing in his life. I think somewhere he said there were two roads to salvation, one was the religious route and the other was the sexual. Well, I don't think of sex as a liberating force. Lawrence, it seems to me gave it an unholy importance. I understand his attitude, which was one of revolt against the morality of his time, but he went too far; he made a gospel out of sex and created a following which made him look ridiculous. He was always at odds with his disciples and probably repudiated them all in his heart.

Lawrence, if he had ever read me, would probably have been disgusted with my kind of writing, the way I use sex in my books. He would never have used the language I did. When you read what he has written today, it all seems so innocent, so puerile. He never employed the language of the man in the street. There was a bit of a prude in him. Perhaps there is in me too. I don't trot out this vocabulary of the gutter unnecessarily. There is a time and place for it. Or the right mood. I don't talk fuck, shit, prick, cunt all the time, as a truck driver might. Intellectuals tend to use this kind of language for effect. I hold them in contempt.

I'd like to go on record as saying that I don't know the answers as to why people do this or that. I don't think one does anything deliberately or for reasons that are apparent. The things we do are for reasons far deeper than we pretend and much more obscure.

This chart indicates why I failed to finish this book on D. H. Lawrence. I got lost in a self-created jungle. I decided that the only story I could tell was my own. In the process of writing some 800 pages I made the sad discovery that my idol was not the writer I had imagined him to be.

May 1912, according to Murry, when he met the woman who was to be his wife "who enters now into the very substance of his work and remains in it to the end" marks the end of the first period of L's life and work, and the beginning of the second. Of these clearly marked period there were four. The first ends with his mother's death; the second begins with his meeting with his wife and ends with the end of the War; the third begins, roughly, with his leaving England in 1919 and ends with his abortive return to England at the end of 1923; the fourth and last period ends with his death, on March 3rd, 1930.

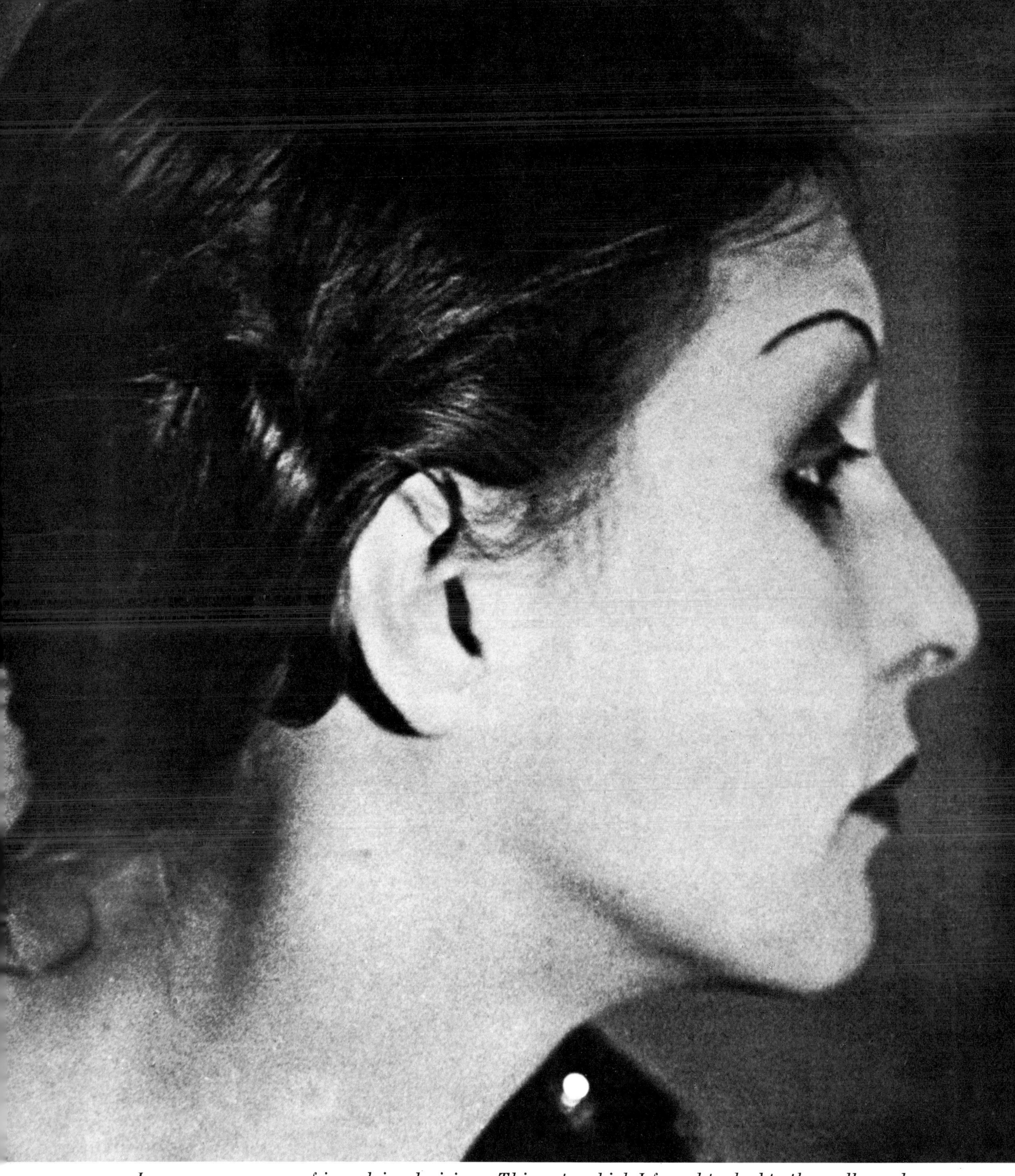

June was a woman of impulsive decisions. This note which I found tacked to the wall one day ended the tempestuous and unbelievably romantic relationship of almost a decade.>

June came over twice or three times, at intervals, for a few weeks at a time. We were still married when I was living in Clichy. It was in the year '33 or '34. In '34 I moved into the Villa Seurat; my book came out the very day I moved in – *Tropic of Cancer*. By this time, June had already left me.

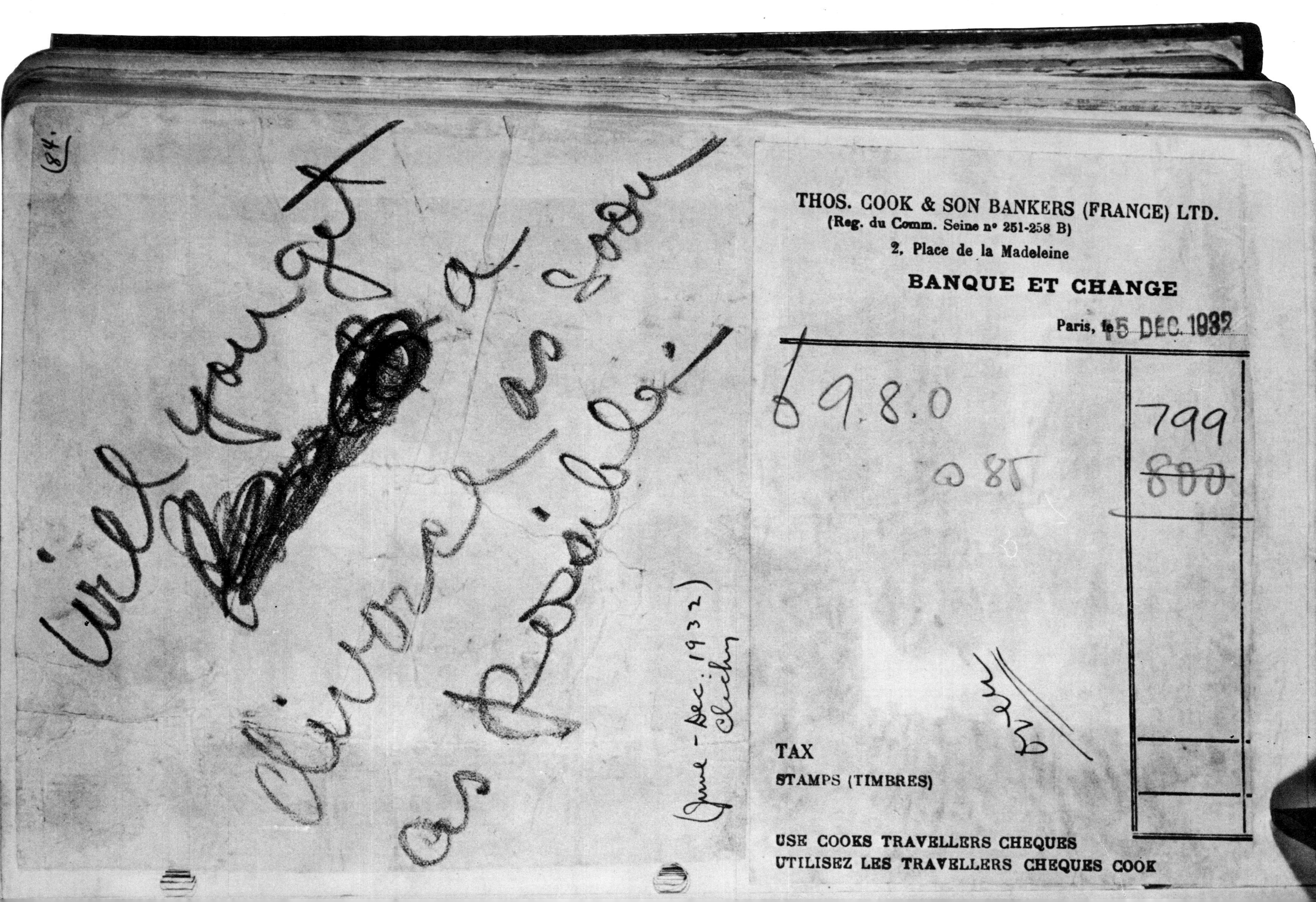

(84.
will you get a divorce as soon as possible.
(June - Dec. 1932)
Clichy
THOS. COOK & SON BANKERS (FRANCE) LTD.
(Reg. du Comm. Seine n° 251-258 B)
2, Place de la Madeleine
BANQUE ET CHANGE
Paris, le 15 DEC. 1932
TAX
STAMPS (TIMBRES)
USE COOKS TRAVELLERS CHEQUES
UTILISEZ LES TRAVELLERS CHEQUES COOK

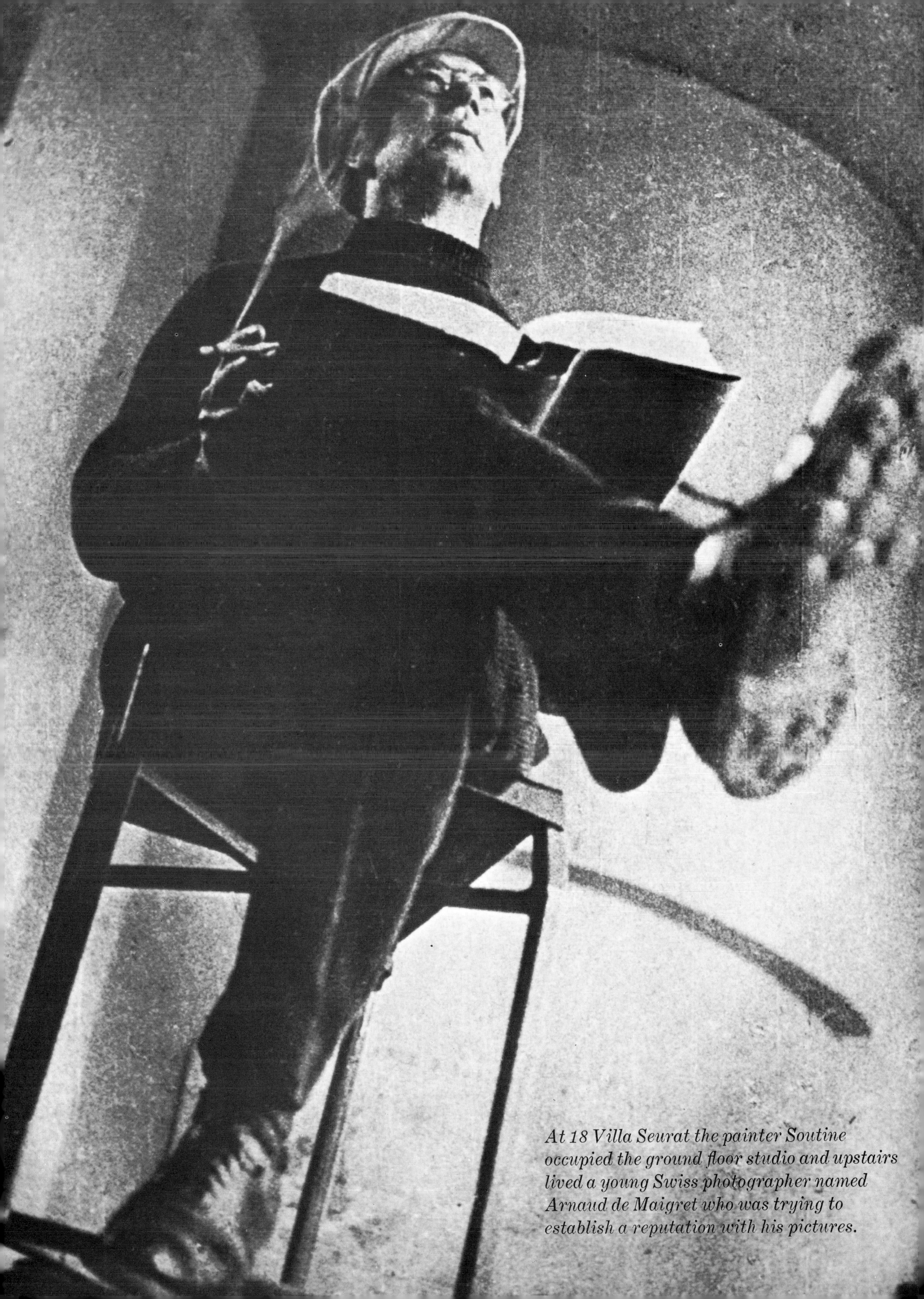

At 18 Villa Seurat the painter Soutine occupied the ground floor studio and upstairs lived a young Swiss photographer named Arnaud de Maigret who was trying to establish a reputation with his pictures.

Black Spring

Reminiscences of toilets ...
Sitting opposite the Dance place (Wilson's) — on steps of comfort station next to kiosk. Then on steps of theatre, opposite "N. V. A." — the great afternoon life on Spring day — the cunts, the bums, the movement, the despair and futility. NEW YORK

Toilets: Wiping ass with "Little Caesar" in French — "Passions" series at 6 francs! Quote chapter headings and occasional lines. What I think of contemporary American literature — toilet paper!

I suffer from a uterine hunger. Was born under-nourished — with a voracious and insatiable appetite. This in connection with Tante Melia — eating dung — bringing her food and a drop of Kümmel'

Everything seemed so much easier there. Here in California distance is a big factor. Even maids have to have cars here. There in Paris no one I knew owned a car. To take a cab—even that was an event. The whole atmosphere was different. There wasn't such a thing as alienation or lack of communication. We were always in touch with one another. I was an exile in a foreign country, which in itself gave me a feeling of great freedom.

The man I conversed most with in Paris—we had *fantastic* conversations—was Michael Fraenkel, with whom I wrote the *Hamlet* letters. In the early days he put me up for a little while at his place. Fraenkel was quite a businessman. He played the stock market, and also made a small fortune selling books.

He was a writer and a poet. He was a very intense man, endowed with a brilliant mind. In many ways we were made for each other, especially when it came to talk. The studio I lived in for the last four years in Paris I rented from him. He lived downstairs on the ground floor. Often he would wake me up to have breakfast. I'd fix breakfast—he didn't know how to do a damn thing—and we'd start talking. Then I'd fix him lunch and dinner! Maybe it would be midnight before he would leave. Needless to say, these were *exhausting* talks.

He had a pet subject, and that was death. He wrote a book called *Bastard Death*. Fraenkel's idea, his whole idea, was that we have to live things through. You have to go through the tunnel until you're in the light again. He would say that the only death is death-in-life, not real bodily death. This was his main theme. He had many themes. He was a metaphysician and a logician. He was a nephew of the Yiddish Shakespeare, and he had that kind of rabbinical mind which cuts with a razor's edge.

During the brief period I worked as a proof reader on the Chicago Tribune's Paris edition I bought a bicycle. This not only took me to work every night but to places like Malmaison, Louveciennes, St. Denis.

From Paris I went to New York and then to Hollywood. This is my last appearance in a Borsalino or any other hat.>

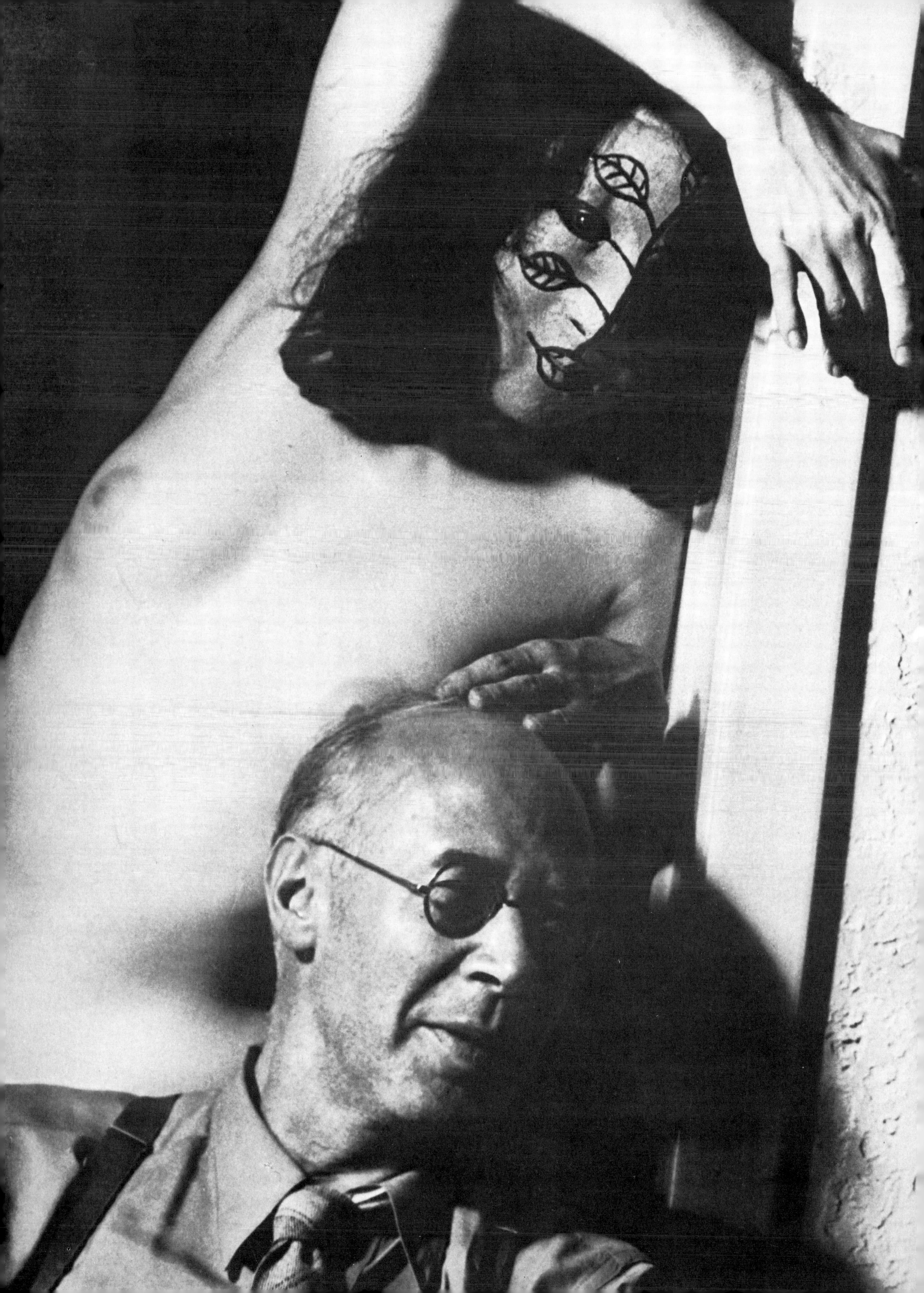

And how we disagreed! That was just it. The whole book, *Hamlet*, was one continual argument – for almost a thousand pages. He was the kind of person who believes one can win an argument. As for me, I played the game. My one concern was to fan the flames. I enjoy talk for talk's sake, come what may. Fraenkel always wanted to be sure I understood his words – "Do you follow me? Do you get it?" And so on. He behaved like a teacher.

We were in contact for a good five years. Then he left France and went back to America where he died. The war was coming on and each year people thought it would happen the following year. This went on for four or five years. Each year a new body of exiles would return to America, afraid that war would happen overnight.

Antonin Artaud – what a wonderful figure in those days – already quite mad when I had my first meeting with him. I was sitting on the terrace of The Dôme with a group of friends, my back to the curb. We were laughing heartily over something someone had said. Suddenly I get a whack on both shoulders with a stout cane. I turn around and it's Artaud. He thought we were making fun of him.

I knew Leger quite well. I don't recall how I met him but I do recall that he would make dinner for me sometimes in his New York studio during the occupation. Abe Rattner I first met in Paris, but I don't recall how. We became close friends. I regard him as a great painter. I knew Matisse's son, Pierre, the one who has the art gallery in New York, but never met the old man. I met Miro briefly much later in Majorca. And then there was Soutine who lived right downstairs from me in the Villa Seurat. By that time his Bohemian days were finished. He was suffering from stomach and liver troubles and whatnot, and lived like a recluse. I used to go down to borrow a knife and fork or salt and pepper from him now and then. Once in a while he came upstairs to my place when we had a party. He had an obsession about Rembrandt, whom he idolized.

During my Hollywood period (1940-42) I met Man Ray, the already famous painter-photographer. During a relaxed session at his studio he shot this candid portrait of me. There was nothing posed about the photo. I didn't even know that the masked nude was behind me. By the time I was aware of her hand on my head the picture had been taken.

I hadn't really chosen Paris to live in. When I left New York in 1930, it was with the intention of going to Spain; but I never got there, not 'til many years later. No, I had no thought of living in Paris. I had been there, about two years before, and I wasn't terribly impressed with it. I think that when you suffer deeply somewhere, anywhere, and you can't escape, you learn to accept the situation. And then you discover marvelous things about the place. Thus, in the midst of my poverty and suffering I really discovered Paris, the true French spirit and many, many other things for which I am eternally grateful.

It's a hard thing for some people to understand, how one can enjoy life when living at the bottom of the pile. Yet I think that that is the most important thing that ever happened to me, to be without anything, no crutch of any kind, cut off completely from all help. You have to *find* it every day, this help; you have to learn to live from day to day. Sure, you suffer and you're miserable, but it's so interesting and so fascinating that you become thoroughly alive. You live by your instincts, just like an animal. That's a great thing for us over-civilized people to know, how to be a bird of prey, an animal, wolfing every meal, begging, being humiliated time and again, accepting it, being pushed down and then bouncing back again. Each day you get through is something of a miracle.

I got very little money out of the *Tropic of Cancer* when published in France. It sold very slowly at first. It was only when the GI's came over and discovered the book that it began to sell in large numbers. By then Jack Kahane was dead. He died the day war was declared. His 17 year old son, Maurice, took over the business. He was unable to send me money during the war – it was forbidden to send money out of the country. We had no correspondence either during that time, but a few months after the war ended I received a letter from Maurice. I have recounted the story many times – how I was living in a little cabin down by the ocean, a cabin that I paid $7 a month rent for. It was one of the convicts' shacks. Then comes this letter saying that there is something like $40,000 in royalties due me. Would I come and get it, because it was still impossible to send it. But I didn't go. I was already on bad terms with my wife, and the thought of going to Paris with her, seeing it after all those years with someone who didn't see eye to eye with me on anything, well, I decided it wasn't worth it. I'll take a chance, I said to myself. The money won't run away.

In the meantime, a good friend of mine, the then consul general in Los Angeles, Raoul Bertrand, heard of the situation and he said he would look into the matter for me. Finally I got part of the money, and with this sum I was able to buy the house in Big Sur which I still own.

When I returned from Paris, I found my father dying. He was dying slowly from cancer of the prostate. I came back from Europe as poor as when I left. I thought my mother had no money, but I discovered later that she had quite a bit stashed away. She never let me know about it and always behaved as if they were penniless. For instance she wouldn't even let my father buy cigarettes; she said it was bad for his health. Imagine – a man dying of cancer, what difference would it have made? I had to sneak cigarettes to him. In that period when he was dying, I really got to know my father as never before. We got to understand each other thoroughly. He was a man who had many friends; everyone spoke highly of him.

Then came time to make the trip that later became "the Air-conditioned Nightmare." I had committed myself. Abe Rattner, my painter friend from Paris, was going with me. Doubleday had agreed to publish the book. In Natchez, Mississippi I got a telegram saying my father was on his death bed. I took a plane immediately but arrived in New York too late. He died in a Jewish hospital. The old family doctors we had had all died off and my mother had to call in a Jewish doctor. In my mother's mind, it was horrible to think that he had to die in a Jewish hospital. It appears he died happily. In his last moments, he told the nurses what a wonderful son I had been to him, which wasn't altogether true.

My first encounter with death was seeing a dead cat in the gutter. I must have been about five years old then. I really think that was my first big shock – seeing that stiff cadaver which was already rotting away. There are other vivid memories too, like sitting by the window when convalescing and watching the snow fall softly against the window panes and tracing patterns with my finger in the frosted window panes.

Death. It has become intriguing to me because in the past ten years I have become sharply aware that one day I am going to die. Till then I hardly ever thought about my own death. How do I feel about it? What do I think about it? Well, nobody knows anything about death! It's a complete blank. No one ever came back from the grave. I have such great, great faith in life that it's difficult for me to think of the absence of life. I regard death as a transition from one form of existence to another. There may be such a thing as reincarnation, but if so I don't think it is as

Tuesday Oct 25/32.

Dear Henry: Recd your Birth day Card in due time. nice card. looked like hand painted. Mother was getting anxious to know if you thought of same. while I am writing this to day, I am holding it over until to morrow A.M. When the Europa comes in perhaps. there may be something in same to answer & then I can mail same in the evening on S.S. New York it sure was a long wait from you, thought you might be traveling. in Reference to your birth. you were born on a Saturday. Mid Day. between. 12 30 to 12 45 cant remember exact. time (1) Dont Know Theo Schaeffer address. in refence to looking up our ancestors. all I Know is that My Father. Hanover. in a town named Minden. " Mother. all I Know. is that she was from Bavaria. & Mr Nieting. was what they called a flinda. Hess. form in. Hessia Darmstadt. Some Day. I may get in touch with Theo Schaffer & find out more. on Mother side. as yet mother has not given me the Details. about your inquiry how to make Kartofel Klaess. & Etc. keep on asking about same. & you will eventually get it I hope you are on the Job. & all is well with you. Enclosed you will find letter from Walter Pach. how do you feel about writing to the Gross. Boys. Whose Mother still lives on our Block. she comes in to visit us. about twice a week. we play cards. with her & her Second Husband. a Mr Troutwein address. Major Felix Gross. Newport. R.I. " Charles " Washington D.C. (will finish this letter in the morning if I receive any mail from you) we are all OK. with Love from all Father.

3 P.M. Wed. Still no mail. So will let this go at that. it looks very much like Roosevelt

By 1932 I had become keenly interested in astrology and in my own horoscope. I was not sure whether I was born at high noon or at midnight. I wrote my father for the information because my mother no longer had any interest in me whatever.

people imagine. What we see is transformation. We don't see annihilation. One thing changes into another. I have no fears about death. Sometimes I even welcome it. I lie in bed sometimes, when I'm feeling very good, and say, "Now is the time to die. I feel beautiful, fulfilled. Let it come now. I'm ready for it."

So I've gotten to live with it, like a companion in waiting. You remember that when St. Francis was dying, he said, "Brother Death, I forgot all about you. I must write a poem to Brother Death." What a wonderful way to die! That's a little bit how I feel about it.

PARIS
REVISITED

After a visit to No. 18 Villa Seurat, where I wrote "Tropic of Capricorn" and several other books, I'm reflecting on the unforgettable days and nights I spent here. In every house along the street called the Villa Seurat there lived a well-known painter, writer, sculptor or musician, among them Gromaire, Lurçat and Salvador Dali.

<Here we are in the miniscule studio of my old friend Brassai, on my left. Here he stores the thousands of photographs of Paris which have made him famous. Everything is in order.

With my then secretary in Paris, revisiting old haunts—during the shooting of the film "The Henry Miller Odyssey."

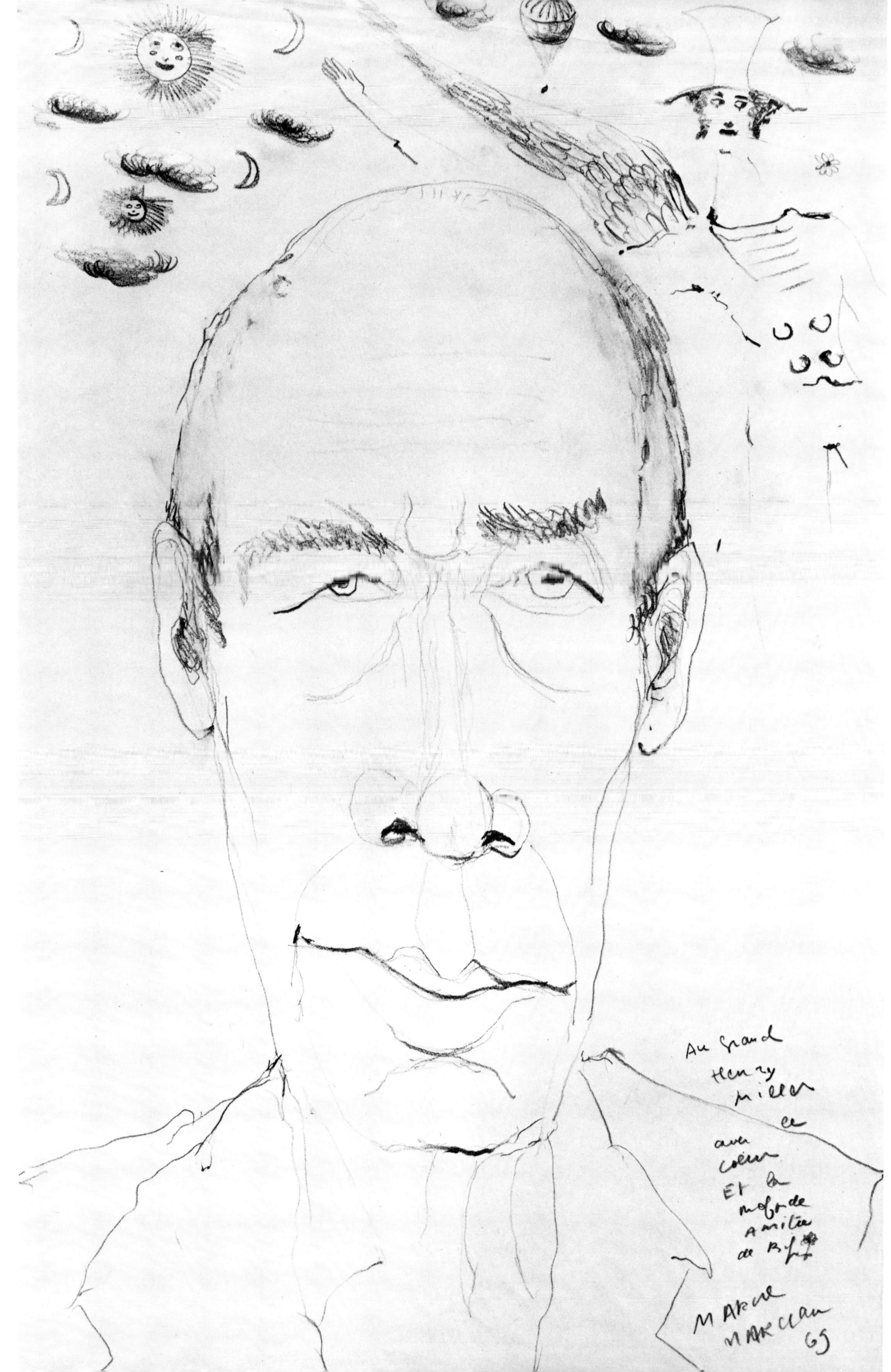
Au grand
Henry
Miller
avec
cœur
Et la
amitié
de Bip
MARCEL
MARCEAU
65

Paris Notes

14th: A dance in the streets with Olga. Bulgarian style, hands around in a circle, good Turkish rhythm. Olga smelling like fried potatoes, her hair greasy and flying in my mouth. Has she bugs? One of those wild Circassian haircombs! Hair like a bunch of excelsior. Coming away from the dance Olga's drawers come down. She ducks into an alley and hoists them up. Explains that since the operation (abortion) she is not so big any more. (She still weighs a ton.)

14th of July: Tameness of it. French don't know how to take a holiday. Americans + other foreigners made it lively. Only two bright spots in the celebration were the blind man playing classic music on the accordeon at Montparnasse, and the solo male dancing in the little family group in dirty cafe back of rue de Lappe, where the music was composed of bag-pipe and sleigh-bells. The whore at Select, trying to gather a crowd by raising her skirts and doing belly-dance. No go!

Lawrence Durrell puts on fake moustache and beard to impersonate Bernard Shaw—in the Luxembourg Gardens, Paris.

I took Hoki-San to Paris for my fifth honeymoon. We only seem to be going in different directions. Actually East and West got together very well.

Number 6.

Note recurrence of this number throughout life.
Mother's birthday — June 13th — (6th month)
My date Dec. 26th, 1891. Born on 86th Street, N. Y. (85th = !
Next address 662 Driggs Ave. Brooklyn.
Born when father was 26 years old. His birthday is Oct. 23rd (twice 3 = 6)
Next address is 1063 Decatur St. B'klyn.
Married in 26th year! Wife lived on 9th Street (6 upside down)
June lives on 1577 76th Street, Bensonhurst (Joey + Tony)
Wife B + I live on 6th Avenue Bklyn. where I am divorced.
Pauline lived at 366 Decatur Street.
Stanley, my oldest friend, lived at 284 6th Street, Bklyn.
Anais at 26 Rue des Marronniers, Paris.

Reflections caused by recollection of number 6 in dream of Brooklyn—Paris map. "Bklyn 6 times as large as Paris!"

In Chinese culture 6 is the 2nd important number after 4, the cardinal for the ~~seasons~~ ("The 6 powerful extremes") (mythological)

Find Colors, Symbols for Topographical maps of

(Life) Driggs Avenue = Boy Heroes, gods, Idol worship
Philos. + (music) Decatur Street = Cora, Pauline (Frances Hunter, Louise Carmen
(Adventure) Sixth Avenue = B—, Muriel, Camilla
(Literature) June period

Color Scheme

Driggs Avenue — Royal Scarlet, Violet
Decatur Street — Blue, Green, Brown
Sixth Avenue — Purple, Violet
June Period — Orange, Green, Yellow, Black, Blue

< In Paris while reading a Chinese book on metaphysics I became aware of the recurrence of the number six in my life.

> Something done in an idle moment for my Danish publisher, Hans Reitzel, while staying at his home in Copenhagen in 1953. Probably under the influence of Rimbaud.

∨ A feeble attempt to imitate Georg Grosz, the German artist, after looking at his famous album of water colors called "Ecce Homo" which I first saw in 1928 and which inspired me to start painting.

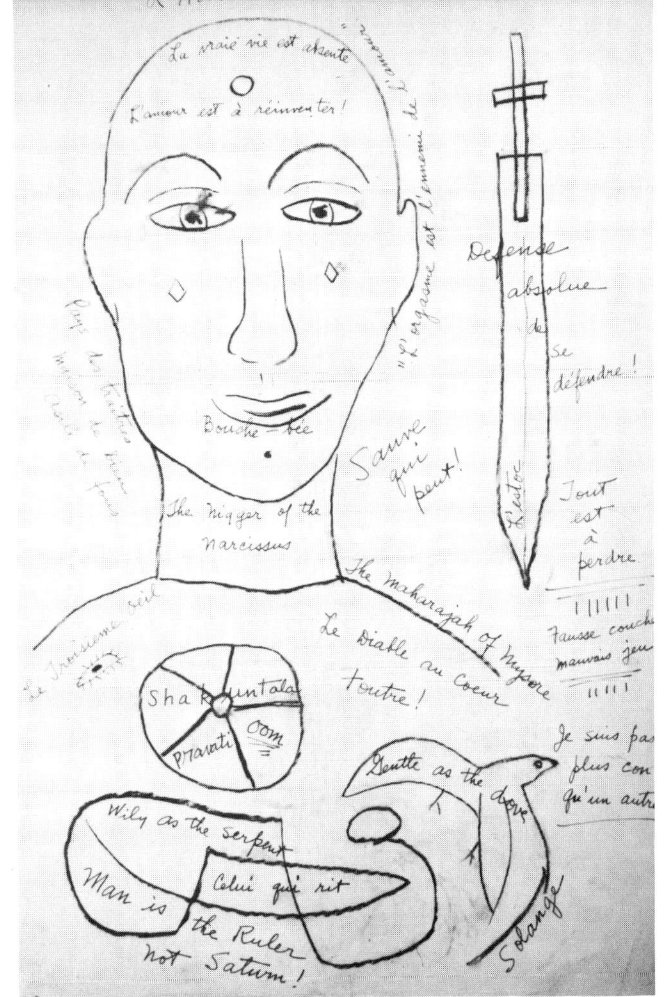

Rue Mouffetard (See old letters)

Eglise St. Medard = organ playing, altar ablaze.
Crowds streaming in — flags flying — Jeanne
d'Arc celebration. Outside tremendous hubbub
markets — newstand with salacious literature
"L'Ami du Peuple" — cries. Turks + Arabs buying fruit.
Walls — blue, mauve, battleship gray, yellow, bilious
crimson splurges. Meat hanging on pegs or lying
exposed on marble or zinc slabs — birds, rabbits
heads, brains, horse liver, rolls of fat, goose grease,
Intestines, head hanging up by brains. Goats herded
outside church — shepherd flaying them with whip,
falling on them like a football player making a
tackle. Gendarmes watching in amusement.
On the corner a group of street singers — girl
playing drum, one singing, 2 accordions. Shivering
in cold rain. Good air this time — sentimental
French song.
Parades starting from Place de Lacepede —
boy + girl scouts — pushing thru the congested
Rue Mouffetard.
Finding section June + I explored when searching
for 2nd hand bicycle — right near Eglise
St. Etienne du Mont — Rue St. Genevieve — hilly,
full of Impasses. Place Lucien Herr, and
Passage des Patriarches = Val du Grace Quartier
In the garden of Eglise St. Medard = street cleaner
in corduroys, eating bread, big bottle of wine. Jew
alongside of me reading Jewish paper. Old woman
with beard + mustache, red eyes, wrinkled, wooden
shoes, and a beret.
Streets off Rue Mouffetard, choked with people.
Black windows — very very ancient, dilapidated.
Stuff for sale seems like the loot of vandals,
or the loot of ghouls who have robbed the graves.
Saws with pink and orange handles, old shawls
old women's hats, shoes again — frightfully worn!
The French sell anything and buy everything.
Not necessary to go to Boul. Richard Lenoir —
the rag + bone market. This is good enough!

∧ *At a writers' conference in Edinburgh Lawrence Durrell, at my right, primes me for the speech I am about to make.*

∨ *The French actor Michel Simon asks for my autograph—the least I could do for him. Twice he lent me his house in La Ciotât, France.*

> *This is Eugene Pachoutinsky, the first of many persons who saved my life in Paris during the dog years. He fed me, kept me in Gauloises Bleues and arranged for me to sleep in the cinema Vanves where he was the ticket taker. He has remained a friend.*

∨ *I requested this photo of Brassai and Picasso because of the amazing resemblance between the two.*

as a younger boy though,
before I was ten, back
in the old neighborhood,
we would pay a girl
a penny and try to
fuck her. We made
believe. It tickled
and felt good.

CHILDHOOD

I remember me at all ages pretty well. I remember the years of one to nine as being my "Paradise" period. That's when I lived in the old neighborhood in Brooklyn, called Williamsburg. At the turn of the century, 1900, we moved to another neighborhood. I was just ten years old. That was the "Street of Early Sorrows," as I called it, in a German-American neighborhood in the Bushwick section. I was going to grammar school then.

What I remember chiefly about that period was that I had to meet a whole new gang of fellows and get along with them. I had trouble with them because they tried to make me the butt of their jokes at first. Soon, however, I became their leader. The first time I walked down the street someone put a chip on my shoulder. Kids did that then. They would put a chip on your shoulder and you were supposed to defy someone to knock it off. If you didn't you had to fight. I refused to fight, which was considered to be pretty bad. I told them that I didn't know them, that I had nothing against them, and that I couldn't see any reason why I should fight them, any of them.

There was a Presbyterian church in the neighborhood which I joined because they had a military brigade for youngsters. It was called Battery A, Coast Artillery. We had uniforms, we drilled according to the manuals and I rose eventually from a private to first lieutenant. This was for kids from ten to fourteen. There were a number of churches like that that had these boys' brigades. It was my sole reason for going to church. I didn't give a shit about the sermons. It was the only religious organization I ever joined.

The streets were still of cobblestone and the automobile was a novelty. I recall some wonderful days in the autumn in empty lots in the neighborhood. We would dig caves in them. Some days we would shoot sparrows and roast them over a fire. I had a 22 caliber rifle, a Winchester. Most of the kids had guns. There were no restrictions about that and people didn't get shot very often.

We would get some of the girls into a cellar and watch them piss. Could they piss up to the ceiling or as far as we could? Things like that. But we didn't fuck them. As a younger boy though, before I was ten, back in the old neighborhood, we would pay a girl a penny and try to fuck her. We made believe. It tickled and felt good.

I remember this too; these were my learning days. I received great instruction in the open lots. There was a fat boy called Louis. He was older than any of us. He used to tell us about strange things, legends, myths, stories that had magic in them. I learned more from that boy than I did in school. We talked about everything. We were curious. Now kids seem bored, don't know what to do. We would ask questions like "Who made God?" "How come the Virgin Mary?" and such like.

When I finally got through high school, I was about seventeen then, we had a club called the Deep Thinkers. The title was ironic. There was a fellow among us who was very silent and he was really stupid. But we always pretended to him that he was very wise because he didn't talk much. We all knew he wasn't, of course. Hence the name Deep Thinkers. Then there was another group from a different neighborhood, Greenpoint, Brooklyn. We were mutual friends and we decided to merge. We

This beautiful photo of the family was taken by the well-known photographers, the Pach Brothers, in New York. They had photographed every President of the United States almost back to Lincoln's time. The elder Pach never used money. He exchanged his photos for everything he bought.

formed a club of twelve fellows and called it the Xerxes Society. The Xerxes Society didn't do anything and the name didn't mean anything. It was just an excuse for us to get together. We had all finished high school and none of us went on to college. We all were musicians: some played the piano, some the fiddle, some were very good singers. Once every two weeks at one or another's house we played and sang all night. Think of it, how different from today! This went on for two or three years. We had little buttons made and we had a handclasp we gave each other. Our parents supplied the food and drink when we met at one another's homes.

We didn't need girls then. Now and then we would have a big party and play post office, which meant taking the girl to a dark hallway to feel and kiss. None of us was then going steady with a girl. I must explain. It seems strange that I had no sex life at the time but that's because I was so madly, passionately in love with my high school sweetheart. Yet I never went steady with her.

This is the graduating class at P.S. 85, Brooklyn, in 1905. I am the third on the left. I can still remember the names of most of these pupils, viz. Jack Lawton, Lester Prink, Morton Schnadig, Lester Faber, Joe Maurer, Jimmy Pasta. The only one with whom I ever kept in touch, and still do, is Jimmy Pasta, son of a cobbler, who became a Congressman. Although my books are known all over the world I have never heard from any of these classmates except Jimmy Pasta.

That lasted three years! And it was a tremendous thing. Every evening after dinner I walked to her home and back again. It took me almost an hour to reach her home, and all I did was walk past her house to see if by chance she might be at the window. It was mad, mad, mad. Three years it lasted. I couldn't look at another woman, I couldn't think about it. All I could think of was her. I never made it with her because I had put her on a pedestal.

About this time I had three or four bouts with whores. In fact, it was during my last year in high school that I paid my first visit to a whorehouse and immediately got the clap. It was on 34th Street just west of Herald Square. There were a lot of whorehouses on that street and most of them had French girls. Later I went back again to the same neighborhood but not to that same whorehouse. It was just my luck to pick up another dose. I had it two or three times.

When we were 18 and 19 years old, we had this Xerxes Society and enjoyed ourselves like kids. I played the piano up until I was 25. I married the girl who taught me piano. That finished the piano lessons. There were two or three of us who kept the spirit of the group alive. It was wonderful later to reflect on this. There were the sluggards, the active ones, the jokers, the ambitious ones. I can see it all so clearly now. I and another fellow were the clowns who entertained them when things lagged. The excitement would die down and nobody would come up with anything—the members were falling asleep. My bosom friend and I wanted so much to keep the club going that we practically stood on our heads to amuse the sleepers. We would put on a kind of vaudeville act, dance a jig, sing a song, tell jokes, make up a skit, anything to keep the others awake and interested. How naive it all seems today.

At eighteen I started working for the Atlas Portland Cement Company as a clerk. That was my first job after leaving school. I gave piano lessons after work for 35 cents an hour. At the home of a little girl whom I taught I met an attractive widow who was a friend of this girl's mother. That's how my first affair began. It was a semi-romantic thing, but of course utterly different from that first pure love. But I had a great deal of feeling for this older woman. I lived with her happily for a while; I even rented a piano and moved it into her place. I was 19 then.

A strange thing was that while living with the widow my old sweetheart lived across the yard. She had already married and was now living opposite me. I didn't know it, of course, until some time later.

After high school I tried City College in New York for about six weeks. What broke my back was Spenser's *Faerie Queene*. I said if I had to read stuff like that I give up. Then about two years later I decided to become a physical culture instructor. I went to Sargent's School of Arms on Columbus Circle. The course took four years, but I didn't last long because my father was drinking and my mother begged me to go and work with him so that I could protect him.

During that period I was in tiptop shape physically. I had become a nut about health and physical culture. Every night I did my exercises. I was also a bike fiend. I had two racing wheels that I had bought at Madison Square Garden from the racers after the Six Day Races. I used to set the pace for them when they worked out. It was fun for me and they used me because I was young, had a good heart, and didn't care how I killed myself. It's not easy, you know, to set the pace. This racing took place on the beautiful gravel path from Prospect Park to Coney Island. It was six miles going and a long six miles back.

Be against! Do something! Do what? Why, for one thing, you might eradicate every weapon, destroy every machine for making weapons. Wipe out, at one stroke, your armies & navies, by simply refusing to serve. Be militant! Don't wait till it's too late! Don't wait for war to be declared by the cabinet ministers before you protest. Start now.

* *

at the age of 18=19

In a way I was influenced by other physical culture nuts at this time—like Charles Atlas and Bernard Macfadden. I'm a frail fellow but I had lots of vitality. Then came a period when I went to wrestling matches to watch men like Jim Londos and the Man of a Thousand Holds and Strangler Lewis. I also attended the fights. Jack Johnson, Stanley Ketchel—I used to watch them train. I never saw Jack Johnson fight but I met him years later—40 years later to be exact. He was the host at a little bar on the Rue Fontaine in Paris. Even 40 years later he still seemed to be in marvelous condition. He didn't look dissipated. You know that massive statuesque head of his. I have a picture of him, now, on my bathroom wall. He was my idol.

Then the walks.... I would get off at Delancey Street on the elevated line. From there I'd walk to Fifth Avenue and 31st Street. It was a good walk—took me almost an hour. All this time I was plagued with the thought that I was a writer who never did any writing. I had made just one attempt to write. With a little broken pencil I wrote half a page and quit. I thought I would never be able to write. Nevertheless, it was there inside me; I would compose stories and novels as I walked, complete with characters and dialogue. Like that I must have written several books. I'm talking of the period when I worked for my father in the tailor shop.

For several years we spent our summer vacation in Narrowsburg, N.Y. on a farm owned by the man on the left. I never again ate so well and so heartily.

On my way to and from the tailor shop I would stop before a certain shop window, a framing shop, where I saw my first Japanese prints. I also saw reproductions of Chagall, Utrillo and Matisse. That was the beginning of my interest in painting. All this time I kept telling myself that I'll never be a writer. But I was reading all the current writers of the day. For instance I remember John Dos Passos who had quite a name already. We were probably the same age and already he had made it. He had been in the war and had written a book about the war. Reading his work I would say to myself, "Jesus, I think I can do as well as that," but I never even tried.

It was after I left college that my real education began. I began to read what I wanted to read, what I was hungry for. I wanted to know about everything then. I read all kinds of books—philosophy, economics, religion, anthropology, anything and everything.

I was really a divided type. I was very much interested in sports but at the same time very literary-minded. I read constantly and would always select the heaviest books. I was an enigmatic figure to my companions. I competed in everything they did but they didn't compete with me. They thought I was an eccentric. Finally I weaned myself of all of them.

When I was a child I was sent to Sunday School by my parents. They really had no religious beliefs. They were baptized Lutherans, but, I never saw the inside of a Lutheran Church. My parents never talked about religion. They never went to church. I never had any interest in church either.

Usually I would sit through the Sunday sermon bored to death. Now and then the minister would invite a minister from another congregation to preach the sermon. I remember one Sunday when I came home from church electrified. I had heard a preacher talk about Socialism. To be a Socialist was to be a real radical in those days. I came home from church and told my parents how wonderful this visiting minister was. When my father heard the word "socialism" he was ready to crack me. He said, "Never mention that word again here." You see, my father was different from my grandfather. My grandfather was much more of a radical than my father. He had fled Germany to avoid military service. He went to London and worked for ten years on the bench. There he became a union man, and he remained one all his life. But my father had become a boss tailor and that made all the difference in the world.

Already at the age of 21 I had reached a point of utter despair. I'm sitting in the park in Union Square, New York. I see a big sign, "phrenology." I had exactly a dollar in my pocket. The sign said it cost one dollar to have one's head read. So I go up and get my head read. The phrenologist, an old lady, feels my head—and what does she tell me? "You could become a good corporation lawyer." I went away utterly disgusted, crestfallen. I had thought she would say, "You're going to be an artist, a writer." I didn't know where to go, whom to look up to. I hadn't the courage to knock on the door of some great man to ask for advice.

I used to hear John Cowper Powys lecture for ten cents at the Labor Temple in New York. A most cultured man and a wonderful writer. He had the face of a seer. Later, some 40 years later, I paid a visit of homage to him in Wales. I told him what he had said to me when I attended one of his lectures in the early days. I was very shy and awkward then. I had gone up to him after the lecture and, not knowing what better to say, I had asked him if he had ever read Knut Hamsun. He replied, "Knut Hamsun, the Norwegian writer, you mean? No, I'm sorry I haven't. You see I don't read Norwegian." When I saw him in Wales and related this to him he said, "Henry, what a prick I was! Why didn't you give me a good kick in the ass?" His books had a great influence on me.

Another man who had a good deal of influence on me was an ex-Evangelist named Benjamin Fay Mills. He used to lecture on all sorts of subjects. Freud, for instance, who was hardly known then to the general public. He conducted special classes which cost $100 a course. When he announced these special lecture classes I said, "I have no money but if anybody is worthy of being in your classes I think I am." He looked me over and said, "I think maybe you're right. If you will pass the plate around for the collection after my lectures, I'll let you take the course free."

There were many men like that whose doorbell I would have liked to ring and ask them a few questions as do my fans now. I have to turn most of them away unfortunately. In the beginning I felt guilty if I didn't listen to them, but today I think I'm really doing them a service by not listening to them. Youngsters can ask all manner of questions, often profound and disturbing ones. I discovered eventually that, after giving time and attention to them, what I said made no difference. I maintain that advice is futile. One must find out for himself. It sounds cruel, but it isn't.

You have to get to the point of no return before you come up again. There's no God protecting you. In the end you have to come back to yourself. It has got to be *you* doing something, whatever you decide upon. Do what you think you have to do and don't try to follow somebody else's pattern because he was successful. You can't be that way. You are you. You're absolutely unique and each one has his own destiny. We can learn as much as we wish, listen to the greatest masters and so on, but what we do, what we become, is determined by our character.

It is possible to transmute the bad into the good, the wrong into the right. There is always this possibility. It would be an utterly uninteresting world if everything remained what it seems to be. I do believe in transmutation. For example, two men are put in prison. One man is utterly despairing; if released he may commit murder again. The other man goes through some inner change and comes out a new man.

I'm 21 years old and still living with the widow but I'm itching to get out of it. I realize that she is older and it worries me. I can see her at 50 and me only 25. So I run away to California. I go out and work on a fruit ranch down at Otay and again at Chula Vista for about six months. I was burning brush in the orchard and there were some cowboys among the workers who became buddies of mine. One was from Montana, and we became great pals. One day he suggested taking me to a small Mexican whorehouse he knew in San Diego. There was a trolley, like the Toonerville Trolley, that ran from Chula Vista to San Diego. On the way to the whorehouse I see posters announcing that Emma Goldman is lecturing on Nietzsche, Dostoevsky, Ibsen and so on. That was a decisive moment in my life. I went to hear her. After attending a few of her lectures, I decided I wasn't fit to lead the life of a cowboy. That's what I had decided to be, *a cowboy*. Imagine! So I returned home and went to work for my father.

My relations with my father were rather cool while I worked in the tailor shop. My mother had hoped that I would prevent him from drinking, keep tabs on him and all that, but I couldn't. He bothered me, disturbed me, getting dead drunk every day. It was only later, when I married for the second time and had all kinds of financial difficulties, that I'd appeal to my father for aid. He believed in what I was doing though he never read anything I wrote.

My father in his prime. At this period I was able to fit into his cast off clothes, whether sack suits, tuxedos or cutaways.

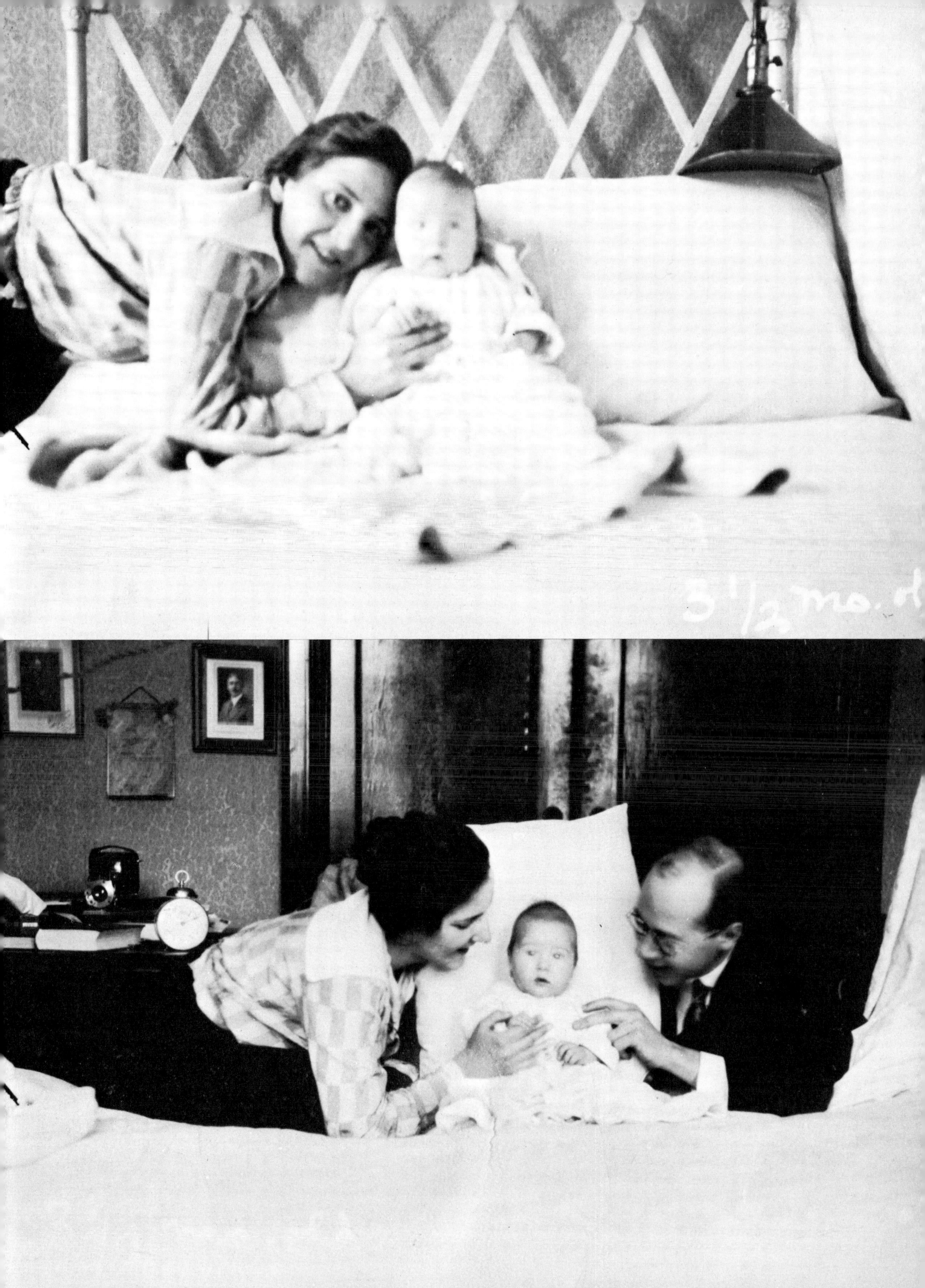
3 1/2 mo.

While working for my father, I married—my first marriage—and had a child. Nights I would sit at a big pigeonhole desk taken from the shop. Also from the tailor shop I had swiped a big mahogany table, a round one, around which a dozen people could be seated. It was pure mahogany, a beautiful table, and I would often sit there and try to write. Not with any success, of course.

I hadn't seen the widow since I went west. I had run away from her and she didn't know where I was. One night I walked into a movie and she's there with a flashlight as an usherette. She escorts me to a seat, sits down beside me, and starts to weep. "Harry," she said—she always called me Harry—"how could you ever have done that to me?" I told my wife about meeting her—she had known all about the affair—and I suggested that we bring her home to live with us. Of course my wife couldn't see it. But I was really sincere. I meant it thoroughly. It was one of those impossible situations which only a fool like myself could imagine would work out.

I think it's quite possible for a man to take care of more than one woman. Yes, on condition that the parties concerned realize fully what they are in for. A lot of primitive societies have done it, more particularly in cases where there was a shortage of either men or women. A friend of mine thinks that a man should take care of as many women as he can keep happy. But then there are economic problems, no?

I never told you much about my father. He was drunk every day. He usually went to the bar across the street towards noon to have his first drink. By the way, it was a wonderful hotel bar—the Wolcott Hotel. He wanted me to grow up, take over the business. He'd invite me to lunch with him and his cronies at the hotel. I'd have gorgeous lunches but I never drank a thing. I never took a drink in those days. I was against it. I would stand at the bar with him and all his cronies laughing and jeering. "Henry," they'd say, "what are you drinking today?" And I'd say, "Water." Then they'd laugh. I would get furious, naturally.

Here is my daughter Barbara with her mother and father. I was 26 or 27 years old and had considerably more hair than now. There are hardly any photos of me extant which show this much hair.

Barbara on the kitchen tubs at 244 6th Ave. Brooklyn

I remember once having a fight with a Frenchman who insulted my father because my father was drunk. He had been calling him all sorts of names. I went up to him and grabbed him. They were all drunk now and in my eyes were nothing but a bunch of bums. I was in fine physical shape and I grabbed him by the throat, banging him against the bar. Then I got him down on the floor and began choking him to death. They had to tear my hands away. I almost choked him to death. I tell you this little story to let you know how violent I can be. I'm afraid to get angry, that's why I'm so nice and peaceful. When I lose my head I go completely haywire.

I was supposed to learn how to cut patterns and all that, but I never did. Instead, I used to stand at the cutting table and talk for hours with the cutter while my father lapped it up at the bar. Customers appeared only at rare intervals.

This cutter was a Jewish immigrant from Poland whom I liked very much. I mention him in my books. We'd stand there and talk while he'd trace patterns and cut. He was supposed to be teaching me, but I never learned. He was interested in literature. He knew Russian and Yiddish literature very well. He told me all about the ghettos of Europe, the folklore, the Kabala and so on. We delved into all manner of things, talking for hours every day. Sometimes I'd go into what was called the busheling room. There were three Jews there who were very interesting to me. One was an opera singer. I would open the windows so that they could hear him in the neighboring buildings. I'd say, "Now, Rubin, start with Pagliacci, or with Boris Godunov." What a voice! Sometimes I think he may have had a greater voice than Caruso. We'd hear them clapping from all the windows roundabout. "More! More!" And if my father happened to walk in drunk or a customer walked in, they'd wonder what the hell was going on.

The business didn't prosper, of course. It went to hell. The wonderful thing was, when it did go to hell and my father was left without a penny, these little Jewish tailors who worked for him offered to pay his debts; they offered to pawn their belongings, give him their savings, and so on. I urged them not to, it was too late. But that's how wonderful they were. It was a great experience.

In the tailor shop I met one of the most famous writers of the day. One day, who steps out of the elevator but Frank Harris. He was led in tow by Guido Bruno, then a big shot in Greenwich Village. Bruno was from Yugoslavia and ran a magazine in the Village.

Photo of my first born child taken on a table in the backyard. She was then about two years old and a very happy child.

He had discovered Frank Harris who was living on Washington Square. Frank Harris needed some clothes. My father, of course, never heard of him, but I had read several books of his and was tickled to death to see him. My father wasn't used to dealing with writers and artists except for Boardman Robinson, the cartoonist. My father had no use for artists. He thought they were all cracked-brained, penniless, irresponsible. Frank Harris wanted a suit of light, gay material for a yachting trip. My father shows him some material with broad stripes—something only a minstrel would wear. Frank Harris begins to laugh. He says, "You mean you want me to wear trousers like this?" and my father says, "Why not? You're a writer, you're a bohemian. You can wear anything."

Frank Harris was really great. He soon discovered the little tailors at the back and noticed that the cutter was a very wonderful man. He got to talking about Jewish literature, Shakespeare, the Bible, Oscar Wilde. He spoke to these little tailors as if they were his equal. They said to me afterwards, "Who is that man? He must be a wonderful, great man!"

I used to help Frank Harris put on his pants when he came for a fitting. He never wore any underwear, which my father thought very odd. I often acted as errand boy after working hours. One day my father asked me to deliver a suit to him. When I arrived at his home there was my beloved author in bed with a woman. I wanted to bolt but he insisted on trying the suit on. He jumped out of bed completely naked and tried the pants on.

I spoke to him about my writing and later he published one of my stories in a famous, old magazine, *Pearson's*, which he had taken over. Later, when I came to Paris, Frank Harris invited me to stay at his home in Nice—rent free. I never accepted the invitation. But how nice of him!

All that I got out of those two, three or four years at the tailor shop was a knowledge and feel of woolens and silks and a few meetings with Frank Harris. I know a good piece of material when I touch it. And I know when a suit fits properly. But that's about all.

Being born in Brooklyn of parents who didn't have anything to do with artists, I never met any. I fought to meet anyone with any culture. To me being a writer was like saying, "I'm going to be a saint, a martyr, a god." It was just as big, just as far away, just as remote as that. For years I only dared dream about it. I didn't even think I had the ability, but it was the one and only thing I wanted to do. Yet to do it I did a thousand other things first.

My father never changed the letterhead after I left the firm. I received this letter in my early days in Paris. I had been away from the firm over ten years.

~~I~~ most people dont think
that Speech of Al Smith has
done Roosevelt much good-
You notice the Democrats
dont let Garner do
much Speaking: most
people think he is a joke-

its rumored that
Tammany is making a
deal- to get O'brien elected
& Kneife- Lehman- for
Donovan-

Business in general-
is not as good this
Month as it was in
~~Sept.~~
regards from Uncle Dan
& Eddie I met them
at Carnegie Hall the other
day they are looking forward
to a letter from you

M ______ TO HENRY MILLER & SON, DR.
Tailors and Importers
FOUR EAST 53RD STREET TELEPHONE PLAZA 1316

Notice I am ~~Chie~~ using these file heads
in order to save my letter heading.

What do you hear from June.

Hello Henry - money ~~got~~ from me as I only
... money they ~~owe~~ owe

I was a street car conductor, garbage collector, librarian, insurance man, book salesman. I worked in the telegraph office. I had just been fired from one of the first few promising positions that I was able to wangle in a mail order house. I was made an assistant editor. I had only had the job for a month. The man above me liked me immensely. He was a literary man. I hadn't written a line but he felt that I was somebody. I learned the job so quickly that there was hardly anything for me to do. So I have Nietzsche in front of me, whom I'm then passionate about, and I'm copying out excerpts from his *Anti-Christ;* suddenly the vice-president walks through, looks over my shoulder and says, "Very interesting, and what connection does this have with your work?" I was caught red-handed, fired.

I had a wife, a child, a household to take care of, so in desperation I go and ask for a messenger job in the Western Union. I'm about 28. I ask for a job as a messenger and they turn me down. That so incenses me that I can't sleep. I get up the next morning and I go to see the president of the company. I was referred to the vice-president's office. I say to myself, "Why, why can't I get the lowest job on earth, a messenger boy?"

I was finally sent to see the general manager who listened to me for an hour or more, and instead of being offered a job as messenger he says, "Mr. Miller, why don't you take over the Personnel Department, be the employment manager. But first, in order to acquire experience, put on a uniform, work as a messenger, and I'll switch you from office to office. You'll get paid as the employment manager. Nobody will know it but we two, but you'll work as a messenger." So I went from office to office and got the lay of the land. Then I discovered what that life was. To tell you the truth I could hardly stand it. It was winter, snow and ice on the ground. I came home the first night as though my feet were made of broken bones and glass. I went to bed groaning with the pain.

Four and a half years I suffered as employment manager. After I finished my day's work I would eat dinner with the detective of the company. He would arrive at closing time and we'd go out together to visit the telegraph offices and look for crooks and runaway boys. That brought us into every nook and corner of New York: the Bowery, the East Side, the West Side, Harlem, everywhere. I knew it all like a book. I was due at work every morning at eight. I seldom arrived on time. When I did arrive there would be a whole mob waiting for me in the anteroom, all waiting to be hired. I seldom got to bed until two in the morning, three or four sometimes. In those years I did the work of three men at least.

I learned a lot of course about human nature, especially about boys. We had largely the scum and the riffraff of the city. There were great kids among them. Lots of them were crooks but I didn't mind it too much. But they were great liars, many of them. Nearly all young kids are liars. The model ones who looked so beautiful and pious were always the worst. I often visited their homes at night to find out what was what. Kids would come begging for the job and say they had nothing to eat at home, their father was ill and this and that, and I'd go visit their homes. Then I'd try to get the charitable organizations interested. They took ages to do anything. The result was that I was paying out of my own pocket to keep them going. I often had to borrow from my associates in the office. I was always in debt. I owed everybody, trying to help these kids.

I hadn't yet come to that point where I resolved to live another life. There were a lot of things that happened first. In the first place I fell in love with a young woman whom I met at a Broadway dance hall, was caught in bed with her by my wife, and divorced. So I went to live with her, June. While I was living with her I quit my job. She kept saying, "Look, give up that job. Start to write." She pushed me into it.

One day I walked into the office, took all my belongings, put them in a briefcase, and said to my assistant, "Tell the boss I'm quitting right now and that I don't want my two weeks' salary." The office was full of boys waiting to be hired; there were always 50 or 60 milling around. It was sheer pandemonium. I walked out that day and felt that I was a *free* man. I deliberately walked up Broadway, it was about ten in the morning, observing all the poor buggers with briefcases under their arms, soliciting, buying, selling, praying and

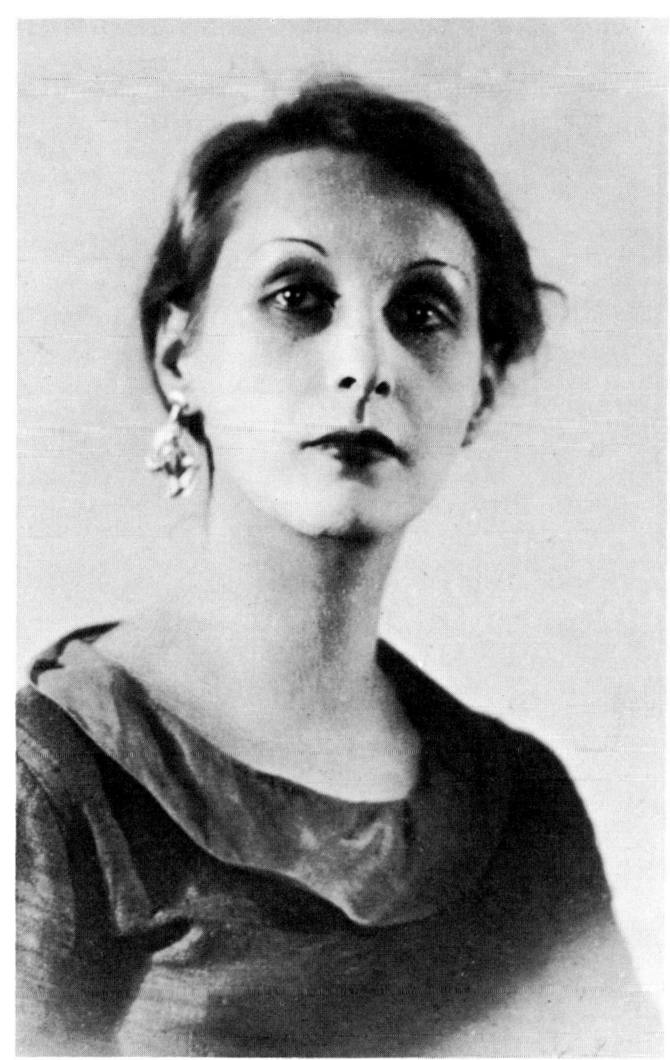

begging. I said, "Never, not for me. I'll never do this. From now on I'm going to be a writer, and I'll live or die by it."

It was because of my wife, my new wife, June, that I got the courage to make these decisions and to live up to them. She really buoyed me up, really helped me. She believed in me. Then began the period when I really did suffer and starve until my first book came out.

I've usually been involved with one woman at a time, almost seven years each time. After separating from June, I became more promiscuous. But while living with June I never went with any other woman. I was so completely absorbed in her, so completely happy with her, especially sexually, that there wasn't another woman who could tempt me.

But then began my ten years of misery, trying to sell my work. This desire to write must have been strong in me from way back. But I had no confidence in my ability to write, that was the thing. I had *absolutely* no confidence. I thought I would start with exercises. I'd write about things I was interested in—people and events. I'd go to meet people. I visited the editor of Funk & Wagnall's Dictionary, Dr. Vizetelly. I wrote an article—a long, beautiful article about words, which I sold to *Liberty* magazine, that 5¢ magazine. They liked me there. They almost gave me a job as assistant editor. They paid me—I think $300—which was a big sum in those days. But they never printed my article. I would ask about it every now and then. "It's too good," they would say. *Too good!* How do you like that? Finally I caught on to the idea of trying magazines like *Snappy Stories* and their ilk. I wrote one or two, had no luck, and then I decided to send my wife, who was beautiful, to see the editors. Then, of course, they sold. After I sold two or three, I thought, "Why should I write new things? I'll go to their back files, pull their published stories out, change the beginning and the end, and the names of the characters, and sell it to them. Naturally they loved this, their own stuff. I sold a number that way.

We moved to 91 Remsen Street, Brooklyn Heights, where we really got started. That was a beautiful place. Aristocratic, you might say. We lived in Japanese style. Everything had to be aesthetic. We were living as though we *had* money; we didn't pay the rent for about four months. The owner of the place and his wife were Virginians. One day he knocked on the door—I was alone—and supposedly writing. He said, "Mr. Miller, could I talk to you?" He sat down on the bed. "Mr. Miller, you know my wife and I are fond of you and your wife. But I think," he said, "you're a bit of a dreamer. You know we can't go on forever keeping you. It won't be necessary to pay the back rent. We know you don't have any money. But would you please vacate in a reasonable time?" So lovely, this man. I really felt bad. I told him I would certainly pay him back. "You've been so kind," I said. Of course, I never did. My wife wasn't working any longer and I wasn't selling anything.

Because of extreme poverty we had to separate for a while. I went back to live with my parents and she with her parents. That was frightful. My mother would say, "If anybody comes, a neighbor or one of our friends, put that typewriter away and hide in the closet. Don't let them know you're here." I stood in that closet sometimes for over an hour, the smell of camphor balls choking me. That way she didn't have to tell her neighbors or relatives that her son was a writer. All my life she hated the idea of me being a writer. She wanted me to be a tailor and take over the tailor shop. Writing was like a crime I was committing.

Even the earliest memories of my mother are unhappy ones. I remember sitting by the stove in the kitchen on a very special kind of chair and talking to her. Mostly she was scolding me. I don't have pleasant memories of talks with her. Once she grew a wart on her finger. She said to me, "Henry," (remember I'm only four years old) "what should I do?" I said, "Cut it off with the scissors." The wart! You don't cut off a wart! So she got blood poisoning. Two days later she came to me with her hand bandaged and she says, "And you told me to cut it off!" And BANG, BANG, she slaps me. Slaps me! For punishment. For telling her to do this! How do you like a mother who does that?

My sister was born mentally retarded; she had the intelligence of a child of about eight or ten. She was a great burden in my childhood because I had to defend her when the kids called "Crazy Loretta, crazy Loretta!" They made fun of her, pulled her hair, called her names. It was terrible. I was always chasing these kids and fighting with them.

My mother treated her like a slave. I returned to Brooklyn for two or three months while my mother was dying. My sister was down to a skeleton. She was walking around with pails and brushes, mopping the floor, washing the walls, and so on. My mother seemed to think that this was good for her, that it gave her something to do, I suppose. To me it seemed cruel. However, my mother had put up with her all her life and there's no doubt but that it was a heavy cross to bear.

You see, my sister couldn't attend school because she was so backward. So my mother decided to teach her herself. My mother was never meant to be a teacher. She was terrible. She used to scold her, crack her, fly into a rage. She'd say, "How much is two times two?" and my sister, who hadn't the faintest idea of the answer, would say, "Five, no—seven, no—three." Just wild. BANG. Another slap or crack. Then my mother would turn to me and say, "Why do I have to bear this cross? What did I do to be punished so?" Asked *me*, a little boy. "*Why is God punishing me?*" You can see what kind of woman she was. Stupid? Worse than that.

The neighbors said she loved me. They said she was really very fond of me and all that. But I never felt any warmth from her. She never kissed me, never hugged me. I don't ever remember going to her and putting my arms around her. I didn't know mothers did that till one day I visited a friend at his home. We were twelve years old. I went home from school with him and I heard his mother's greeting. "Jackie, oh Jackie," she says, "Oh darling, how are you, how have you been?" She puts her arms around him and kisses him. I never heard that kind of language—even that tone of voice. It was new to me. Of course, in that stupid German neighborhood they were great disciplinarians, really brutal people. My boy friends, when I'd go home with them, would say, "Defend me. Help me. If my father starts to hit me, grab something and let's run."

I had no real contact with my mother when I was grown. I saw her briefly when I came back from Europe after being away ten years. But after that I had no contact with her until she became ill. Then I went to see her. Still the same problem—we had nothing in common.

I was about 14 at this time. My father was then at the height of his career as a Fifth Avenue tailor. My sister is beside him. This summer we spent our vacation at Lake Pocotopaug, Connecticut.

Father + Lauretta,
about 1905–07

Weighed 185 lbs.
now is 110 "

The horrible thing was that she was really dying this time. (You see, once before I had gone to see her when she was supposed to be dying.) She lasted three months before passing away. That was a terrible period for me. I went to see her every day. But even when dying she was that same determined tyrannical person dictating what I should do and refusing to do anything I asked her to do. I said to her, "Look, you're in bed. You can't get up." I didn't say you're going to die, but I implied it. "For the first time in my life I'm going to tell you what to do. I'm giving the orders now." She rose up in bed, thrusting out her arm, shaking her finger at me. "You can't do that," she yells. There she was, on her deathbed, and I had to push her down with my hands around her throat. A moment later I was in the hall sobbing like a child.

Sometimes now in bed I say to myself, "You have reconciled yourself with the world. You don't have any enemies. There are no people you hate. How is it you can't conjure up a better image of your mother? Suppose you die tomorrow and there is a hereafter, and you encounter her. *What are you going to say when you face her?* I can tell you now she'll have the first and last word.

A weird thing happened when we were burying her. It was a freezing cold day with the snow coming down thick. They couldn't get the coffin angled right to lower it into the grave. It was as if she was still resisting us. Even in the funeral parlor, before that, where she was on view for six days, every time I bent over her one of her eyes would open and stare at me.

The years between the taking of these two pictures, one in my sixth year, the other in my eightieth, have been good to me. Anyway it's a beginning don't you know.

ACKNOWLEDGEMENTS

I am grateful for the assistance given me by the Special Collections Library of the University of California at Los Angeles. A special thank you goes to Robert Snyder for locating and supplying certain photographs and to his colleague Baylis Glascock for the use of several transparencies taken by him. I appreciate the cooperation of the following photographers who have kindly given me permission to use the pictures they took of me on various occasions:

Jose Alemany, 155
George Barrows, Hollywood, 163
Brassai, Paris, 178 (bottom right)
Wynn Bullock, Monterey, 89
Larry Colwell, 88, 95
Baylis Glascock, 24, 25, 29, 170, 171, 174, 175
Edgar w. d. Holcomb, San Francisco, 18, 19, 31
Tom Hormel, West Los Angeles, 17
Winston Kao, Hong Kong, 32
Arthur Knight, Petaluma, California, 94, 97
Christian de Bois Larson, Beverly Hills, 22, 23, 60
Judy Longini, Sausalito, 85 (column 2)
Fred Lyon, Sausalito, 85 (column 1)
Arnaud de Maigret, Paris, 160
Man Ray, Paris, 164
Geoffrey Palmer, Big Sur, 102, 103
Dick Rowan, Big Sur, 106
René Saint-Paul, Paris, 178 (bottom left)
Red Skelton, 43
Helen Paula Smith, 5-7
F. Florian Steiner, 100-101
Teas, Pasadena, 80-81
The Scotsman Publications Ltd., Ireland, 178
William Webb, Carmel, 35, 84
Mary Willis, Edmonds, Washington, 87
Cedric Wright, 90, 91, 96, 97

All contemporary photographs not otherwise credited were taken by Bradley Smith.
I would also like to thank the owners of some of my paintings for allowing their reproduction in the Painting Section.
They are:
Jakob Gimpel, 113, 129, 132
Joe Gray, 114
S. Kubo, Japan, 131
Dr. Jack Sheinkopf, 117, 118, 119, 123, 130 134, 135
Hoki Tokuda, 116, 133, 136 (top)
Paintings on the following pages are in my personal collection: 115, 120, 122, 124, 126, 127, 128, 136 (bottom)

HENRY MILLER

The specially printed end pages include a chronology of Henry Miller's life from birth to the age of 80. The type is set in Century Expanded. All of the handwriting is by Henry Miller. The book was printed and bound in Japan by Toppan Printing Co.

INDEX

INDEX

N

O

P

R

S

T

U

V

W

X

Y

1949 Finished *Plexus*. Began writing *The Books in My Life*.

1951 Separated from wife Janina Lepska; the children went to live with her in Los Angeles. Finished *The Books in My Life*.

1952 Eve McClure arrived April 1 to live with me. Began writing *Nexus*. Divorced from Janina Lepska. Left for tour of Europe with Eve on December 29. Arrived in Paris for New Year's Eve.

1953 Big year — best since Clichy. Invited to stay at home of Maurice Nadeau, former editor of *Combat* and chief organizer of the *Defense of Henry Miller*. Visited Rabelais' house outside Chinon, then to Wells, England, to see Perlès and wife. Took in Shakespeare's house at Stratford-on-Avon, with Schatzes. Flying visit to John Cowper Powys in Corwyn, Wales. Back to Paris. Returned to Big Sur at the end of August. Married Eve McClure in Carmel Highlands, chez Ephraim Doner, in December.

1954 Alfred Perlès arrived in November to write *My Friend Henry Miller*. Traveling exhibition of water colors in Japan. Began writing *Big Sur and the Oranges of Hieronymus Bosch*.

1955 Barbara Sandford, daughter by first marriage, came to see me; hadn't seen her since 1925. Perlès left for London in May. Had visit from Buddhadeva Bose of Calcutta, Bengali poet. Wrote *Reunion in Barcelona*.

1956 Left for Brooklyn in January with Eve to take care of my mother who was dying. While there met Ben Grauer of NBC and made recording *Henry Miller Recalls and Reflects*. Returned to Big Sur. Collection of short pieces translated and published in Hebrew — *Hatzoth Vahetzi* (Half Past Midnight). Finished *Big Sur and the Oranges of Hieronymus Bosch* book.

1957 Rewrote *Quiet Days in Clichy* upon recovery of ms., which had been lost for 15 years. Exhibition of water colors at Gallery One, London. Completely rewrote *The World of Sex* for publication by Olympia Press Paris. Exhibition of water colors in Jerusalem and Tel Aviv. Began writing *Lime Twigs and Treachery* but abandoned it to resume work on *Nexus*. Elected member of National Institute of Arts and Sciences.

1958 Continued work on *Nexus*.

1959 Finished *Nexus* in early April. Left for Europe with Eve and children on April 14. Rented studio on Rue Campagne-Première, Paris, for two months. Visited Danish publisher on trip to Copenhagen with children; Gerald Robitaille acted as "governess." First meeting with Antonio Bibalo, composer of opera *The Smile at the Foot of the Ladder*. Returned to Big Sur in the middle of August. Wrote the three letters contained in *Art and Outrage* (Perlès-Durrell).

1960 Wrote *To Paint Is to Love Again*. Left for Europe April 4 to attend Cannes Film Festival as one of the judges. Spent a few days in Paris, then to Hamburg to visit Ledig-Rowohlt in Reinbek. There met Renate Gerhardt for the first time. After traveling in France and Italy, returned to Big Sur. Returned again to Europe. At Rowohlt Verlag, Reinbek, wrote preface to new edition of Elie Faure's *History of Art* (Gallimard) and several minor pieces, including one in (crazy) German called *Ein Ungebumbelte Füchselbiss* for a little revue called *Rhinozeros*. Also did drawings and water colors for editor of the revue, Rudolf Dienst. Made a number of water colors and played much ping pong at Rowohlt Verlag. With Ledig and others visited Mölln (Til Eulenspiegel's birthplace) and the Luneberg Heide, Bremen and other places. Over Christmas holidays wrote first draft of *Just Wild About Harry*, chez Renate Gerhardt.

1961 Toured Germany, Austria, Switzerland, Italy, Portugal and Spain. Visited Marino Marini, the famous sculptor, who did my head in bronze. Returned to Pacific Palisades from London in November. In this year Grove Press published *Tropic of Cancer*.

1962 Began volume two of *Nexus* while in Pacific Palisades. Took trip to London to visit Perlès and made tape with him for Canadian B.C. (television). Visited